Contents

Ready, Set, Retire!

How to Do the Things You Want to Do in Retirement with Peace of Mind

Paula Dorion-Gray, CFP, CSA

Reality Books
Prairie Grove, IL

Published by Reality Books
2602 IL Route 176
Prairie Grove, IL 60014

Publisher's Cataloging-in-Publication Data
Dorion-Gray, Paula.

Ready, set, retire! : how to do the things you want to do in retirement with peace of mind. – Prairie Grove, IL : Reality Books, 2006.

p. ; cm.
ISBN: 0-9772767-0-8
ISBN13: 978-0-9772767-0-7

1. Retirement—United States—Planning. 2. Retirement income—United States—Planning. 3. Estate planning—United States. I. Title.

HQ1063.2.U6 D67 2005
646.79-dc22   2005933952

Book production and coordination by Jenkins Group, Inc.
www.bookpublishing.com

Interior production by Debra M. Beck
Cover design by R. N. Johnson & Associates

Printed in the United States of America
10 09 08 07 06 • 5 4 3 2 1

Ready, Set, Retire!

The Total Vision Approach™ to Planning
and Enjoying Your Retirement

Foreword

When Germany's Chancellor Otto von Bismarck first put forward the idea of mandatory retirement in the late 1870s, it was to create a system whereby older workers would be replaced by younger ones. This assured that there would be an ongoing, continuous workforce and dissuaded those who might have otherwise opted to become revolutionaries rather than take secure jobs. Bismarck's plan was actually a forerunner of the Social Security system we've come to know, as evidenced by his 1881 letter to the German Parliament in which he stated, *"Those who are disabled from work by age and invalidity have a well-grounded claim to care from the state."*

To retire in Bismarck's time, however, and subsequently throughout much of the twentieth century, was seen as the act of being taken out of use. Ships were retired to shipyards, and workers retired to a life of complacency. In fact, the definition of "retirement" still emphasizes withdrawing.

Retirement:

1. The act of retiring, the state of being retired; withdrawal; seclusion.

2. A place of seclusion or privacy; a place to which one withdraws or retreats.

While some people do indeed look forward to seclusion or privacy, particularly if they have been figures in the public eye, most retirees today would not include those words when discussing retirement. Once thought of as a transition from an active lifestyle to a far more passive one, the term "retirement" has spawned new definitions for millions of Americans. Such definitions include pursuing dreams and goals, starting new ventures, and maintaining an active lifestyle.

In fact, many retirees today are quoted as saying "I can't imagine how I ever found the time to work–there's just so much I love to do."

Therefore, the term "retirement," in this book, takes on a more transitional meaning. Hence, you are retiring from one aspect of your life while moving into another, meaning that you are making the transition. You are now embarking on a lifestyle filled with new dreams, goals, and/or even challenges.

So, what's on your retirement wish list?

Will you continue to work, perhaps at a slower pace?

Travel cross-country in an RV?

Volunteer for a favorite charity?

Build your dream home?

Move to a sunny spot and play golf every waking hour?

Go back to school?

Perhaps you'd like to pack up and head to a big city to soak up the culture you've craved for years.

You may want to stay right where you are to be close to your family and your close friends.

All these options and more are available to you–if you plan properly.

And the time to plan is *now*.

You may think your greatest asset is money, real estate, or your stock portfolio. In fact, when it comes to retirement planning, your greatest asset is time: the weeks, months, and years between today and the day you retire. Whether you begin at 40, 55, or somewhere in between, the more time you have, the better your chances are of creating the fulfilling retirement you've worked so hard to earn.

It's time that lets you shape and reshape your plan until it's just right. Time opens new vistas and sheds light on exciting savings and investment opportunities. Time enables you to enjoy the process of thinking about your future and carefully planning for your retirement.

Yes, it is also time that enables money to grow. No less a genius than Albert Einstein admitted his amazement at this concept. When asked to name the most remarkable principle of the universe, rather than reply with *momentum, relativity,* or *inertia,* he answered compound interest!

Whether you're wondering how to set aside a portion of your $130,000 annual salary or how to invest your million-dollar nest egg, the information contained in this book will lead you to a more rewarding, enjoyable retirement starting today, right now.

For more than 20 years, I have helped hundreds of clients in a variety of age groups and financial circumstances imagine, plan, develop, and implement successful retirement strategies.

Because a successful retirement is about more than money, I view my role not only as a planner but also as a counselor and sounding board. I listen to people talk about their dreams and help them find ways to make such dreams come true. Very often, people are busy planning their finances without thinking about what they will do to make themselves happy. Conversely, others are busy daydreaming about an exotic retirement lifestyle without taking the time and effort to put the practical elements in place. My primary tool is something I call the Total Vision Approach™. This process is designed to help each person plan for this important chapter in his or her life by taking into account both the daily, practical elements and the emotional elements and dreams that will make up the retirement years.

Do I want to move or stay put?

How much should I leave my heirs?

Who should inherit the family business?

Is there a way to leave a lasting legacy for my favorite charities or my grandchildren?

These and other questions are as emotional as they are financial, and although there are many good books on retirement planning—especially when it comes to the nuts and bolts of 401(k) plans, pensions, and investments—few, if any, include the emotional issues surrounding retirement with the financial ones. Today, more people than at any time in history face the choices and decisions of retirement—a retirement that may last longer than their working life. The Total Vision Approach is a powerful ally.

Years ago, retirement was viewed as an end. It was thought of as the end of your working life, the end of your productive time, and the end of your contribution. Today, it marks a beginning. Thanks to a more health-conscious society, coupled with numerous medical breakthroughs, people are living in retirement much longer, and they're filling their cup to the brim with exciting experiences, newfound passions, and exemplary contributions that never cease to amaze me.

I truly believe that retirement can, and should, be a new and exciting chapter in your life, a time of stimulation, freedom, and contribution. Retirement should not be a dreary day-to-day existence. You should be limited only by your own desires, not by your financial resources.

The entire aim of retiring is to have the time to enjoy other aspects of your life. Whether you have been planning your retirement down to the smallest detail for years or whether you began to ponder the possibilities just yesterday, this book can help you get and stay on the path to designing and funding the time of your life.

By picking up this book, you have taken the first step. Now, the sky is truly the limit!

>   — Paula Dorion-Gray, CFP, CSA
>   November 2005

A Note on Clients' Stories

The stories included in this book are composites designed to underscore important points and show the Total Vision Approach in action. The names of the individuals or couples are changed for confidentiality.

Introduction: Forget Retirement: There Is No Such Thing

What does retirement mean to you? The short answer—and the best answer—of course, is anything you want it to mean. In today's world, anything is possible provided that you have the resources to make your heart's desire a reality. The fact is that in the past 20 years, retirement has been redefined and will continue to be redefined as baby boomers and the generations that follow them continue working and living longer than previous generations. According to the American Association of Retired Persons (AARP), in its report *Beyond 50: A Report to the Nation on Economic Security*, people turning 50 today have about half of their adult lives ahead of them.

Today, more than 32 million Americans age 50 or older are in the workforce, and the number is rising. AARP's Beyond 50 report also explains that "pre-retirees and younger retirees view retirement as more of a lifestyle transition than a termination of employment. They expect to be active, engaged, and working either full or part-time."

In short, people approaching retirement today are beginning to view that milestone as the start of a time to enjoy newfound freedom, a time to make new choices and dream new dreams. They approach life after 50 with more education and greater economic resources than retirees of the past, as well as more diverse attitudes, experiences, and expectations of retirement. In every respect, they are reshaping the meaning of the term "retirement."

AARP is not alone in acknowledging the trend toward retirement as an active lifestyle. David Demko, editor in chief of AgeVenture News Service, put it more succinctly, urging his readers to "Forget retirement. There is no such thing." Instead of simply heading off into the sunset, Demko suggests that people retire from their jobs but not from life and encourages them instead to find out what excites them and to pursue it passionately.

While the dreams of today's retirees have changed, so has the financial model on which these dreams are based. The traditional model for a secure retirement has often been described as a three-legged stool, with one leg each for Social Security, individual savings, and employer-provided pensions. But just as easing back into a rocking chair is no longer the model for living a satisfying retirement, neither is the three-legged stool a viable financial model for planning one.

We've discovered that many people will remain actively at work in retirement, either on a part-time or even a full-time basis, making current earnings a factor in financial planning for retirement. Just as important, two of the three legs have melded into one; traditionally defined benefit pension plans have slowly disappeared and have been replaced with defined-contribution plans such as 401(k) and 403(b) savings plans, a change that has deliberately shifted responsibility for accumulating retirement funds onto employees. The battering of the stock market and the 401(k) plans of several prominent companies in the recent past has brought that responsibility and the attendant risk into sharper focus than ever before.

Today's financial model for a successful retirement is a four—not just three—legged stool: **Social Security, pension/savings plans, current income,** and both **health and long-term-care insurance**.

So whether you're in your 40s, 50s, or even 60s, your retirement has the potential to be far different from your father's or mother's in length, activity, and financial flexibility. You may continue to work, start a new job, establish a new business, or find the right balance between work and leisure. Or, you may still simply retire to the golf course or to taking care of your grandchildren a few days a week.

The choices are many, and they are all yours to make. The key is planning and not just financially. There is a need to plan your lifestyle on the basis of your goals and dreams but also a need to prepare yourself emotionally for retirement. I ask people to try to imagine themselves further down the road, having retired years ago. *What were the past 20 or 30 years of your retirement like? Did you do what you wanted to do?* By taking such a perspective, people begin to look more closely at the significance of that increasingly longer stretch of time that will be their retirement years.

It is also important to think about making the transition from a current career to a retirement lifestyle. People generally don't realize or fully appreciate the good feeling they have from holding an important position in a company or having the respect of their peers in the business community until they are away from those aspects of their careers. Even the day-to-day routine, which may not seem like much now, will be missed when a person retires after years of working at a specific job.

The sense of control, the interaction with various people, the immediate response to your phone calls because you are calling as a significant member of a key corporation—these are all little things that can be badly missed. It is important to prepare for retirement and make a gradual lifestyle transition so that when you walk out the door for the last time, you are not just leaving something behind but approaching something with expectations, excitement, and even passion. The emotions that go with the transition from working full time to retirement have to be addressed, and we will talk more about them later.

A Plan with Staying Power

To use an old cliché: "People don't plan to fail; they fail to plan."

Today, the need for a financial retirement plan is obvious. You simply cannot retire in style and pursue your heart's desire without an adequate level of financial resources, and to accumulate such resources, you need to plan ahead.

However, too many of us neglect an aspect of planning that's equally—yes, equally—important: the emotional side, or the part that I call your life plan. "I have come to the conclusion," writes retirement expert Michael Stein, author of *The Prosperous Retirement: Guide to the New Reality*, "that more retirements will fail for non-financial reasons than for financial reasons."

The bottom line: in order to fully enjoy this new phase of life, you've got to prepare emotionally as well as financially, and these two elements of planning must be viewed as two parts of a whole. Too many planning approaches address one or the other, leaving many retirees "all dressed up with no place to go." They concentrated hard on building a nest egg but neglected to think about what they wanted to do with that nest egg.

Think about it. You've worked all your life. Then, the day arrives when you walk out the door for the last time. Perhaps there's a party held in your honor. Lots of fun, good food, laughter about the old days, perhaps an embarrassing story or two. The door closes behind you. Suddenly, the days stretch before you. You've got nowhere to be; Monday is the same as Saturday. If you haven't thought about what it will mean to stop working, how that will affect you, and how you'd like to fill your days with enjoyment and meaning, there's a good chance you'll be bored and confused. Not surprisingly, many people in this position end up sinking into a dull routine that ironically leaves them longing for work.

At the other end of the spectrum are retirees, including many baby boomers, who have great dreams for retirement but limited financial resources for realizing those dreams. Instead of taking that month-long tour of the Alps, they're stuck taking the virtual tour on their computer at home and thinking about what might have been. This is because they did not plan well financially.

Among my retired clients, the most satisfied are not the ones with the most money but rather the ones who knew what they wanted to do in retirement and were able to use their retirement financial plans to implement their retirement life plans. These work together as a total vision for the retirement they've worked so hard to earn.

What will *your* retirement look like?

A Dorion-Gray client, a husband and wife, Bob and Laura (both age 50), had a combined annual salary of $170,000 as well as $250,000 accumulated in a 401(k) plan plus pension income that he will begin to take at age 55. Their goal was to retire from corporate life in five years and move to New England to be near their family. Bob also wanted to continue working in a job where he could reduce daily stress while still having a major impact. Three years after developing a plan, Bob received a buyout offer from his company. He jumped at the chance because the buyout would let him realize his goals without tapping into his 401(k).

Today, Bob and Laura are living just outside of Boston, within 10 miles of their family, with no debt beyond their mortgage. Bob works at a school and helps run the after-school program. He always loved being around children, and with his own children having grown up and his grandchildren living far away, he hadn't had the opportunity. Bob was also well organized and had leadership qualities but was always part of the corporate world, which left little room for innovative planning. Now, at the local middle school, he can plan and coordinate programs, spend time around youngsters, and get some fresh air during the day rather than be cooped up in an office. Bob's dreams were not exotic. They were simply dreams of doing what would make him happy. Laura, meanwhile, also wanted to be around her grandchildren more often. She too was happy to leave the corporate world and took a volunteer position at a local hospital. She was always looking to find the time to do volunteer work, but with a full-time job and her family, she never had the time.

Bob and Laura were able to make their dream a reality sooner than anticipated because they had a sound financial plan in place. When the right opportunity arose, they were ready to take it. They were able to restructure their life so that they would be near their family, stay busy, and enjoy more time spent outdoors. Emotionally, they looked forward to their new lives in a new place. It was a simple plan but one that could work only with planning.

Another client of mine, Diane, a single woman, worked for a number of years for a large corporation. About 10 years ago, as a result of financial constraints, she was let go. Since that time, she worked in temporary accounting positions where she could use her accounting skills. In recent years, however, because of the changes in the industry and new technology, coupled with her age, it became increasingly more difficult for her to find a position.

We sat down and examined what Diane's needs were on the basis of the planning we had done while she was working full time. We were able to show Diane that on the basis of her current income needs, she was in a position to retire if she chose to take that step. Having no partner to share her emotional concern, she decided to continue to work—but on her terms.

Tired of pursuing temporary jobs on a regular basis, Diane was now able to take a job of her choosing. In her case, it was a position in full-commission sales for a furniture company. This gave her greater flexibility and allowed her to utilize skills that she enjoyed but had not used during her accounting career, such as a flair for home decorating. She could pick her hours and work as much or as little as she chose, depending on how much income she felt she needed.

In three years, Diane will be eligible for Social Security, which will likely pick up the portion of the income that she is now earning by working at the furniture company. But it wouldn't surprise me if Diane continued working.

After all, she is working at something she enjoys very much and that fits into her lifestyle well.

Two other clients, Wendy and Chris, both worked for years in the corporate world. Upon retiring, they wanted to pursue their love of history and spend time with their children and grandchildren.

For this couple, retirement was more of the "traditional" kind—no part-time jobs or business ventures. Instead, their life has become very full with short trips, visiting with family, and volunteering at museums and on historical tours of Chicago. In fact, they even sold their home in the suburbs to move into the Windy City. Now, they can take part in the culture and enjoy the history of the great city in which they had spent so many hours busily working in their corporate offices. Chris has become quite the expert on the history of Chicago.

Both Wendy and Chris knew that if they wanted to enjoy their retirement lifestyle, they would have to continue an ongoing plan of investing and saving through their working years. They followed their plan, and it resulted in a very fulfilling retirement.

As you can see, each client sought a slightly different retirement lifestyle, yet the results are the same in one key respect: each created a financial plan and a life plan and set about making them happen together. Everyone realized his or her "total vision."

In this book, I'll describe the Total Vision tools these clients used to build financial and life plans for a fulfilling retirement.

In Chapter 1, we'll take a look at the faces of retirement today, a peek at the creative ways people are living their lives, and the options open for you to create your own "face of retirement."

In Chapter 2, we will explore the emotional issues associated with retirement. Here we discuss the emotional side of retiring and look at several common scenarios and what you can do to ready yourself for the emotional transition.

Then, in Chapter 3, we'll discuss how to plan for retirement by looking at your current expenses and determining what your lifestyle will be like in your retirement years.

Chapter 4 describes the components of a solid retirement plan. Here, I take an in-depth look at several of the areas you will need to address when building your financial retirement plan, including your time horizon, risk tolerance, and the potential obstacles you may face along the way.

With the preliminaries of planning in place, Chapter 5 explains how to develop a strategy that fits your needs, with special consideration for your personal time horizon and risk tolerance. Here, we look at managing your assets, various investment opportunities, and the manner in which they all work together to provide you with your retirement income.

In Chapter 6, we'll discuss estate planning, which includes leaving a legacy. We'll look at the importance of organizing your personal information for your heirs and will even provide a means of doing so. We will also discuss wills, trusts, and charitable giving strategies that can help you have an impact for generations to come.

Finally, it all comes together in Chapter 7 with the Total Vision Approach by going through a case study. We take all the pieces and turn them into one seamless process that lays out goals, identifies potential obstacles, and shows the steps and processes to develop a comprehensive retirement strategy. The complete retirement picture becomes clear, and the pieces fall into place.

My ultimate goal is to guide you along the road that leads to the retirement of your dreams.

Pick your lane—fast, medium, or slow—and drive to your heart's content. Let's go.

NOTE: The following stories and case study are taken from my 24 years of experience as a financial planning practitioner. It is my job to assist my clients in defining their goals and developing a plan that will help them reach these goals. The development, implementation, and monitoring of a plan takes time and commitment from the client and the planner, and results can be linked directly to that commitment. It should not be assumed that the results from financial planning in the future will be profitable or will equal the performance of these clients. The names of the clients have been changed to protect their identities. The client stories are not testimonials or endorsements from the clients, and the stories are not indicative of the results of all clients.

1 Profiles in Retirement: What Will Yours Be Like?

A peek at the creative ways people are living their lives and enjoying each phase of their retirement

What do today's retirees look like?

Look at that couple taking their third European vacation this year. They're retired.

How about that woman handing in her term paper to the professor? She's retired.

Or the man who spends 20 hours a week helping others build new businesses?

How about the woman who just started her own business?

Or the one over there baking cookies with her grandchildren?

Retired. Retired. Retired.

How about that youngish-looking couple playing golf? They too are "retired" from their long-term jobs but not from their dreams and aspirations. They have moved on to a new phase of life.

Finally, how about the 55-year-old who goes to work three days a week at his old company? He takes a lot of ribbing from his coworkers because he too is retired.

At the other end of the spectrum is the woman who walks to the post office once a month looking for her Social Security check to cover the rent. There's the couple who rarely leaves the house and hasn't been out of state in five years because they're living on a fixed income. There's also the couple from New York who had to sell their house and move away from family and friends to a smaller, more affordable apartment in another state. They too are retired but are not able to fully appreciate the wide range of options open to them in their retirement years.

You get the picture.

There are as many faces to today's retirees as there are people. The difference among them is that some have choices and some do not. Some have the financial flexibility to direct their lives while others find that they are directed by the lack of financial flexibility.

Which side do you want to be on?

Over the years, in good times and bad, statistics tell us that only 4% to 5% of Americans will achieve the financial independence necessary for a secure retirement. I do not want you to be among the 95% destined for financial *dependence*, living on limited sources like Social Security and a small amount of personal savings or being forced to continue working to make ends meet.

To make your retirement lifestyle one that fits your dreams and goals, you will need to determine what it is that you want to do and where you want to do it. Then, you must plan effectively, with your specific goals and dreams in mind. And, finally, when you do plan effectively, you enter a phase of life that is full of possibilities: a time of continued challenge and growth, a time of relaxation and enjoyment, or any combination of these attributes. These are illustrated by the various faces of retirement.

Today's retirees are doing more than any previous generation. They are traveling, contributing, learning, and volunteering. As defined earlier, retirement has become a transition from working full time to working at enjoying life in whichever manner best suits the individual: from traveling for business to traveling for joy, from working for someone else to self-employment, from earning a living to building a lifestyle. Those are the new faces of retirement.

The Faces of Retirement Today: What Will Yours Look Like?

So, where do you see yourself when you retire? If you visualize yourself 20 or 30 years down the road from your official "retirement" from your career or job, you begin to realize that there is a long stretch of quality time available that you can fill in with numerous projects and activities. When clients come to me,

I want them to think about the long term, the second halves of their adult lives. Many people never stop to ask themselves the following questions:

What do I see myself doing?

Who will I be spending time with? Family? Friends? New coworkers?

Where will I be living?

Will I be working at some new enterprise or volunteering my time?

Will I be living my dreams and doing the things I've always wanted to do but never had time for?

Will I be conquering new challenges?

Will I be playing golf, sailing, or traveling?

Location, Location, Location

One of the key factors in planning your retirement lifestyle is picturing where you will be living. Nothing is more disheartening than to hear people tell me they wished they could have moved to a place closer to their family or retired to a warmer climate but did not prepare to do so or were disappointed when they got there. Where you will settle down to live once you retire is very significant.

While many people will have suggestions of places where you can soak up the sun or play golf, one of the most obvious choices when planning where you will settle is to simply stay right where you are. By their mid-50s, most people are well established in their communities and have long-standing friendships and perhaps family living nearby. Many people who have a large empty nest still enjoy living in their homes and have turned children's bedrooms into special interest or hobby rooms.

However, for you, the big question, of course, when contemplating staying in your home is, Can you afford to do so? If mortgage payments ate up a large portion of your paycheck while you were working, it may take some creative financing to ensure that your house doesn't overburden your retirement resources. If you want to remain in your house, you may want to take steps to pay off your mortgage completely before you retire.

If you've been comfortable in your home for 20 or 30 years, you might not realize how attached you are to your surroundings. If you are an empty nester, you may be told by friends, well-meaning relatives, and financial advisors to sell your house and buy something smaller; after all, why do you need to rattle around in such a big house? Why? Because it's your big house complete with memories, packed with emotions, and it's the result of years of toiling to pay off that mortgage. Moving from your home is a decision you should make emotionally and not on the basis of saving money, unless you simply have not planned well and can no longer afford to stay where you are.

When people come in and talk about their house as equity, I wonder whether this is really the clients talking or words from some article they've read or a commercial they've heard. Most people do not think of a house as equity but as a home for their families. Therefore, I generally do not like to include the equity of a home as part of a retirement plan. I prefer that people think more about where they really want to go before they even think of selling their home. When a couple tells me, "If we sell our home, we can get $500,000," I ask them where they are planning to go. Often, they haven't thought it through. People don't realize that it's not always easy to just pack up and move. They don't realize that it may not save them any money if they want to continue to enjoy the lifestyle to which they have become accustomed. Popular retirement areas are often more costly because there is a greater demand for homes in these locations.

The bottom line is that people should be heading toward a place where they really want to be and not simply selling a home for retirement money.

Those who do want to pick up and find a new destination are often looking at buying a place in Arizona or Florida. They've seen the brochures, and they like the idea of warm weather and have heard good things about these areas. Perhaps they've visited someone in a retirement community. I recommend that people spend some time experiencing the lifestyle of a potential new location. It takes more than a weeklong vacation to feel confident that they will enjoy living in any new community. I also recommend to people that if they do actually move, they should first rent before buying.

In addition, you need to consider the various factors involved with settling in a new location.

FOR EXAMPLE:

- What type of climate would you most enjoy? Have you had enough of the cold winters?

- Would you be comfortable in a retirement community with people of your own age?

- Would you be more comfortable in a vibrant city with cultural attractions and more activities?

- Would you be comfortable in an intellectually and culturally stimulating university town?

- Are the climate and culture less of a concern because you want to be closer to your family?

These are some of the questions to ask yourself, questions that may take some time to answer.

Every year there is a new "Best Places to Retire" list. For you, however, the most important criteria are what fit on your list. What will make you happy? Consider living, if only briefly, in one of your potential spots, or try to visit it during different seasons.

Of course, some people like to jump in an RV and just meander from state to state or even country to country to their hearts' content. There are even a growing number of retirement communities springing up in northern states for people who care less about the weather and more about being near their families or exploring the culture and enjoying the ambiance of cities like Chicago, Boston, or Seattle. In fact, Dell Webb, the builders of a number of popular retirement communities in and around Arizona, are already building retirement communities outside of the typical "hot spots" for retirees who prefer being near their families even if it means dealing with a little rain and snow.

One of my clients was planning to leave the warmth of Texas for the misty, albeit lovely, city of Seattle to be closer to their son and his family. While this may be a marvelous plan, I did recommend, as I generally do, that they try out the lifestyle for two to three months before committing. In addition, they might make sure that their son is planning to stay in Seattle. He's in his 20s and has talked about relocating his family to California. Therefore, several factors need to be considered before making a major move.

No matter where you choose to settle, moving takes time and careful consideration.

Explore your options carefully

Retirement is a major life change and one that takes time and energy. Therefore, the last thing a person needs is to go through that transformation and at the same time pick up and move to a new location.

Wait a year, adjust to your new "retirement lifestyle," and then, if you have a destination that appeals to you, spend some time in a new location. If you really like it, then consider selling your home and moving.

SOME CHOICES

If you are exploring the possibility of moving to a new location during your retirement, you might want to explore some of the following sources:

Retirement Net, at *www.retirenet.com*, allows you to browse retirement communities on the Web. Communities are categorized into several sections ranging from "Active Lifestyles" to "Golf Communities" to "Assisted-Living Facilities." You'll also find rentals, which is an important feature if you are not yet ready to commit to a new location.

Virtual Retirement, at *www.virtual-retirement.com*, has choices of retirement locations and assisted-living facilities plus retirement news and a mortgage calculator.

Senior Resource, at *www.seniorresource.com*, is appropriately self-billed as an e-cyclopedia of housing options and information on retirement. Numerous articles discuss moving, relocating, and even reasons to stay put. You can look up resources by state and also find legal and financial information and even humor on this comprehensive Web site.

Stay Active; Stay Connected

Returning to that visualization of looking back over 20 or 30 years in the second half of life, there will be a need for most people to feel vital, active, and connected during that time. For that very reason, several women in their late 70s work at Tiffany and Co. a jewelry store in Manhattan. Their husbands worked for many years and in most cases put away sizable nest eggs. Therefore, these long-time Tiffany's employees need not work for a modest paycheck. However, working at this high-end exclusive store provides them with an opportunity to mingle with interesting customers from around the world, remain active, and be part of the workforce. It allows them to feel vibrant and stay connected.

Experts agree that being vibrant and active are key ingredients to a happy and fulfilling retirement. It's not how much money you have, where you are living, or even how you fill your time. It's your *attitude*. A positive attitude typically comes from staying connected to the world and being engaged in activities that interest and excite you.

Retirement expert David Demko has four rules to make sure you stay engaged, excited, and fulfilled in retirement:

1. *Plan to retire from your job but not from your life.* There's all the difference in the world between the two.

2. *Think about what makes you tick, what makes your life worth living.* Some of the people we've shown in this chapter used retirement to engage in a passion or activity that truly excited them.

3. *Set lifestyle goals.* Plan to make your retirement years as interesting as possible. Make a list of 10 things you'd love to do when you retire. If you're not doing these things now, begin to do them on a small scale so when you retire they'll naturally expand into even larger activities.

4. *See through the dollar signs.* Don't get too caught up in the financial aspects of retirement planning. You need a nest egg, no question, but you also need your health to enjoy the lifestyle it affords you. Living a healthy life is your first-class ticket to enjoying your retirement years.

These are all great guidelines and food for thought.

To these I would add one more: *Plan to stay in touch with a strong network of people who support you.* A study at the University of Michigan concluded that the most powerful predictor of life satisfaction right after retirement was not health or wealth but the breadth of one's social network. People who retire need to replace the social connections they enjoyed at work. This means retirees should plan to invest time and effort in meeting new people and staying in touch with old friends. This may also include discovering other venues for meeting people, such as continuing education courses, exercise programs, and volunteer work.

School Is Cool

One of the best ways to stay connected to the world is through school, and school is the perfect place to begin to kindle your interest in a particular subject. You might be surprised to know that older "nontraditional" students comprise a rapidly growing share of college enrollment. In the 20 years between 1970 and 1990, the enrollment of full-time students nationwide age 25 and over grew 164%. And the increase is even more remarkable for women age 40 and over: 235%! Not surprisingly, more and more people are moving to university towns for the energy and the intellectual and cultural stimulation they'd otherwise find only in a major city. Most major universities offer adult education programs, and many have a wide variety of courses. Whether someone plans to use such course materials to help start a new business venture or simply to explore a topic of interest, taking courses is a great way to stimulate the mind. It provides new avenues to explore and offers new topics to discuss. It also opens the door to meeting new people.

Expand Your Hobbies

Many people enter retirement thinking that at long last they can pursue their interest in photography, acting, cooking, woodworking, painting, gardening, or one of a thousand other avocations. If you too have a hobby that is truly a passion, chances are you won't have much difficulty creating or expanding a list of activities based on this interest. There will be clubs to join, contests to enter, classes to take, books to read, and much more.

Many people, however, have been consumed with one thing for 20 or more years—work—leaving little time to develop outside interests.

WHERE TO START?

Contact a local community college that offers adult education classes. You can sample a few of those until you find an area or hobby that interests you.

Go online and look for associations in areas that have always interested you.

Browse the craft or hobby sections of your local bookstore or library for more ideas.

Whether you're searching for a new endeavor or devoting time to your current hobby, retirement provides a marvelous opportunity to explore areas of interest. In fact, it is recommended that you start seeking out areas of interest well in advance of retirement so that you make a smooth transition into something you already have a passion for.

Too often a retiree decides that he or she now has time to take up sailing, tennis, antique collecting, or some other activity that he or she has always wanted to do only to feel disappointed that it isn't as much fun or as invigorating as imagined. However, the person who loves golf but has never had the time to play will feel released from the bonds of work and onto the golf course, already fully aware that this is where he or she was destined to be.

Start looking for hobbies now! They're good for you.

Work

The younger you are when you retire, the more likely you will be to consider some type of ongoing employment. If you retire at the age of 55, you will need significantly more money to live on than if you retired at 65. You may have more expenses such as making payments on a mortgage, supporting children still living at home, or helping parents who need emotional and monetary support. If you plan well, you can make ongoing work a preference rather than a necessity. However, regardless of the expenses, retiring 10 years earlier will require a substantially larger nest egg to support a lengthier retirement lifestyle.

If you choose to work during your retirement, you might be interested to know that you're in good company. In fact, the trend toward early retirement has come to an abrupt end according to the National Council for the Aging, citing a new report from the Employee Benefit Research Institute (EBRI).

Many Americans are leaving the workforce more gradually than in previous eras and are moving from full-time work to "bridge jobs" before withdrawing fully from the workforce. The EBRI study found that one-third to one-half of older full-time workers hold a part-time job or short-term job before retiring completely. The continued desire to work appears to reflect people's preference to stay active and to maintain a vital social network and an income stream at the same time, as evidenced by the women working at Tiffany's, mentioned earlier.

It has also become more commonplace today for a person to retire on a Friday and return to work on Monday as a consultant, commanding good fees and working on a more flexible schedule. It seems that companies are finally beginning to realize that despite many initials after their names and high academic accomplishments, young up-and-comers aren't always ready with all the answers. For that reason, many companies find that the talent and experience that walk out the door when a longtime employee retires are not so easy to replace, and they're only too happy to invite these valued employees back as independent consultants. Other companies are hiring retirees as part-timers. Emotionally, it is important for most people to feel needed and to maintain a sense of self-worth from playing a key role in a business. It's a difficult transition to go from working hard and making important decisions to having little to do and few decisions, if any, to make.

One client of mine sold her business and had a very difficult time letting go. The contract included her being involved during a transition period but not in any decision-making capacity. As the new owners modernized the business with new phone systems and computers, she felt very uncomfortable. Ultimately, the new owners, aware of how hard this emotional transition was for someone who had built the company and now had to let go, sat down and worked out an agreement to end the contract sooner rather than later. It was a necessary parting of the ways for the betterment of all parties. As it turns out, once she was totally removed from the company, there was nothing tying her to her Midwestern location, so she picked up and moved to California, where she became involved in cultural activities, which she always enjoyed. In the end, she was very happy but simply needed to cut the cord and move on. Sometimes that transitional phase is very difficult emotionally, especially for someone who has worked in the same business for many years.

Start a Second Career—or Your Own Company!

Some retirees may work for their old companies while others find a new job or even begin a second career once they realize their experience qualifies them for a variety of positions.

If you're really adventurous, you may want to start your own business. But, keep in mind that this is riskier than any of the above work options and may consume a lot of time and money. Unfortunately, there are too many stories of retirees blowing an entire nest egg on a doomed business venture.

You need to have money specifically set aside for such a business venture or a means of getting backers so that you do not need to tap into your nest egg to get a new business off the ground.

One of the ideas that many of my clients ponder is that of buying a franchise. Jeff, a client who recently retired, started researching franchises as a way to have his own business. He settled on a computer franchise and was told by the company that he needed to invest only $100,000 and in three years he'd be making $150,000 a year.

We sat down and discussed the feasibility of this plan. First, I reminded him that he didn't know anything about computers. Next, I reviewed his portfolio and explained that he could not afford to lose the $100,000. If this didn't work out, he would not be able to get by with that kind of a loss. In addition, we discussed the fact that this company had not been around for a very long time. Jeff felt that he would be getting in on the ground floor of a new venture. While this might have been the case, I reminded him that many young growing companies fail to meet expectations and that this was, therefore, a very risky venture.

While establishing the fact that this was not a good idea, we also started discussing what Jeff was passionate about, what he really enjoyed doing. It turns out that he used to fly single-engine airplanes and enjoyed it very much. He hadn't flown for a while but always wanted to get back to it.

Today, Jeff is a flight instructor, and while he is not making a lot of money, he is doing something he really enjoys and is not risking his retirement nest egg in the process.

I might add that many people want to go down that franchise road. All you need to do is pass a crowded McDonald's or a Denny's and you can see the potential success of a franchise. The reality, however, is that it is a lot of work to make a franchise successful, and you typically need to own several to really make money. In many cases, your success is only as good as your location. In addition, large franchises are usually tightly controlled by the parent company, taking away much of the "joy" of being your own boss—which is why many people buy into the franchise concept in the first place.

Another client of mine was asked to get involved in a restaurant. Someone else would run it on a day-to-day basis, but he would put up $50,000 of capital and be a restaurant owner. While this is a romantic idea, the reality is that it is a major risk and very hard work. To be successful, an owner needs to be there all of the time and stay on top of the investment. Like any cash business, a restaurant requires constant attention. It's a tough business and certainly a major risk for someone who either doesn't have experience in the field or doesn't want to spend endless hours working.

Ask yourself these key questions before you start a new business venture:

1. What sort of business would I start?

2. Do I have the necessary resources to get started or the ability to get funding?

3. How much time would I realistically need to devote to the business to make it as successful as I'd like?

4. How hard do I really want to work?

5. What would be the key ingredients of a viable business plan for this venture?

6. Is my idea for a business something that would attract consumers in the current market?

7. What kind of competition would I be up against?

8. What experts can give me an honest assessment of my business plan? My attorney? My accountant?

9. Can I feel comfortable as the captain of a small, fragile ship? Do I have the patience to watch as a company grows or possibly struggles to grow?

Before starting a business, do plenty of research. It's one thing to have a great idea but another to have a marketable business idea that will bring in money. Put together a business plan that outlines exactly what type of business you are planning to start and provides you with a blueprint of sorts to determine whether it is viable. A business plan will also help you attract potential investors.

You will also want to explore various means of protecting that which you have accumulated. You do not want to lose major sums of money while investing in a risky business venture, nor do you want to be liable for a business that either does not succeed or is sued. No matter how passionate you are about starting up a business, talk with a legal advisor and your accountant to find the best way to separate the business from your personal savings.

Volunteer

When income is not a concern, a great way to remain active and vibrant is to volunteer your time and talents to an organization or group that you care about. The list is endless, and your local library or Chamber of Commerce or the Internet can help you find the organizations in your area that would benefit from your help.

When looking to volunteer, you can be selective. You need not work in a hospital if it makes you uncomfortable or travel to a neighborhood in which you do not feel safe. Whether it's a local library, a soup kitchen, or the local Red Cross, you can find a volunteer opportunity that feels right for you.

In addition, volunteering often allows people the opportunity to explore new skills and to utilize skills that they hadn't been able to use at their jobs. A client of mine who was a former executive left the stuffy corporate world and now enjoys nothing more than doing magic shows for children at a local children's center on weekends.

Remember: the most significant reward of volunteering is that special feeling you get from helping other people.

A Total Life Plan

The term "retirement" has gotten a bad reputation. It still conjures up memories of bored people remembering the past instead of building the future. As you can see by the examples we've mentioned above, it can be so much more. The sections above hopefully started you thinking of possibilities for your own retirement years.

As I noted with the AARP research earlier, more than 50% of Americans reaching the age of 50 will have half their adult life ahead of them. That's a long time, and it makes sense that having a total life plan for staying active and vibrant is critical to living those years well.

Rather than just wealth accumulation, I challenge you to think about your retirement planning in terms of total life planning and lifestyle goals:

- Enjoyment
- Continuing education

- New hobbies
- More of the same hobbies
- A new job
- A new business venture
- Volunteerism
- Relaxation
- Travel

Whenever I recite such a list of choices to new clients, they look at me a little funny. They have been so indoctrinated by the focus on amassing as much money as possible that they have not had the time to focus on all of the life choices that are open to them. It's important to have a reason—or several reasons—for building a nest egg. Plenty of money and nothing to do with it is akin to being all dressed up with no place to go.

Therefore, the idea is to start imagining what a retirement lifestyle will look like and to think in terms of creating it and then work on accumulating the money to make it a reality.

Here's what I tell my clients is the ultimate goal of retirement planning: a long, comfortable, and totally worry-free lifestyle with no compromise and no concern about running out of money—ever.

Your Retirement Lifestyle

At the heart of the Total Vision Approach is an image or a mental picture of the lifestyle you'd like to enjoy in your retirement years. This image is organized around three things:

1. Where you want to live (both the geography and the type of dwelling)

2. How you want to spend your time (this can be one or more vocations or avocations)

3. Your hopes and plans for leaving a legacy (to your spouse, your heirs, or a favorite charity or church)

Now, it's your turn. Fill in some of your retirement lifestyle goals, plans, and ideas.

Take a moment to write in the space below your top five retirement lifestyle goals.

1. _____

_____

2. _____

_____

3. _____

_____

4. _____

_____

5. _____

_____

Bear in mind that your answers may change as time passes. You might, for instance, think you'd like to start a small business when you retire only to find later on that you'd prefer to work for a small company where you can have an impact but no financial risk. The Total Vision strategy includes steps for revisiting your retirement financial and lifestyle goals on a regular basis.

What does all this lifestyle planning mean? It means that retirement is no longer the last quarter in the game of life but more like halftime. It means you have a lot of exciting and meaningful planning to do beyond that of just dollars and cents.

2 The Emotional Side of Transitioning to the Rest of Your Life

Typically, people spend their time focusing on and worrying about the financial side of retirement. While this is certainly worthy of such concern and requires careful planning, there is another aspect of retirement—a significant aspect—that receives far less attention. That is the emotional side of retirement. Sure, the money is important, but as we all know, money alone does not make people happy.

There have not been many studies conducted about the emotional aspects of transitioning to retirement. Most of the studies that have been done show an increasing number of people focusing on retiring to something rather than from something. They are also looking to retire to a lifestyle that makes them feel good inside. The current crop of baby boomers facing retirement is becoming increasingly aware that there may be many years ahead of them. They are looking at more than just preparing financially and at making an emotionally satisfying transition and finding things to do that will make them feel happy, fulfilled, and productive.

Planning Together

You bought a home together, raised the children together, and survived the good and bad times together. Therefore, your impending retirement is not the time to surprise your spouse with your sudden retirement dream of moving back home to North Dakota. From an emotional—and financial—standpoint, you will want to prepare for your retirement years together, facing your possible fears and discussing both the retirement dreams that you share and those that you don't.

Communication is very important for couples approaching retirement, and it ties in very closely with how well they will handle the emotional aspect of this lifestyle change. Talking about individual dreams and future plans is imperative. What kind of retirement lifestyle is he looking forward to? What does she see in her picture of retirement? What will he do with himself every day? How will they get along?

According to Dr. Phyllis Moen, a professor of sociology and human development at Cornell University and the lead author of a study on couples' retirement transitions published in *Social Psychology Quarterly*, the transition from working to retirement is both stressful and emotionally difficult for most couples. In her recent study of 534 married couples who were either retired or about to retire, Dr. Moen found that while retirement itself was a happy time for couples, the transition (defined as the first two years after leaving a job) was a period of marital strife for many men and women. However, statistics did not identify an increase in the divorce rate, indicating that couples did indeed work things out. I would compare this to the first two years of a marriage, when the couple is getting more familiar with the new lifestyle.

Below, we list several fairly common scenarios that couples face, primarily during the transitional period. They provide food for thought, for discussion, for planning, and hopefully for learning. They focus on emotional issues and emphasize the need for communication and compromise.

SCENARIO #1: He's Driving Me Crazy!

He's been the sole earner, and she has been a busy stay-at-home mom, raising the kids and running the household. Perhaps it sounds old fashioned in this day and age of career women and two-income households, but this is still a very common scenario throughout much of the United States. Now, with the kids gone, she has her own circle of friends with whom she plays bridge, shops, enjoys golfing, and is involved in the community. She spends time with her grandchildren, takes classes at night, and has created a fulfilling lifestyle that she thoroughly enjoys. Suddenly, he's home, he's around the house, he has plans for "them," and she doesn't know what to do. "He's driving me crazy" is the familiar refrain around the hair salon where she seeks solace among her friends.

To quote a line from the old CBS hit television show *The Cosby Show*, "A retired husband is like having a grand piano in the kitchen. It looks good, but the damn thing is always in the way."

Retirement doesn't sneak up unless someone in a company walks into the office and hands an employee a retirement package some five to 10 years before he or she is prepared to call it quits. In this situation, planning includes not only what he wants to do when he finishes working but also how that will or won't impinge on her lifestyle. In some cases, she is very happy to spend less time with the girls and do more things with her husband, some of which they've wanted to do for years. However, in many other instances, she does not want to give up the lifestyle she has created for herself. She is, in a word, "happy."

Rather than telling him coldly to "go find a hobby," she might take some time to help him explore which hobbies he might be interested in pursuing. His day-to-day lifestyle is changing in a major way, and he may be very scared. If she can provide support and make some time in her busy schedule so that they can enjoy doing things together while not giving up her overall lifestyle, they may find a happy medium. He, meanwhile, needs to respect that she is already in a good place and does not want to uproot her lifestyle. He, therefore, has to work toward making plans that he can enjoy by himself or with his own circle of friends.

It's a compromise that includes "me" time and "us" time. It should be discussed well in advance of retirement so that the transition and subsequent retirement lifestyle are satisfying for both partners.

SCENARIO #2: I'm Scared

This is similar to the above scenario, except that she's less concerned with her lifestyle changing and more fearful of him retiring for a financial reason. She doesn't want him to retire. She fears that they will not have enough money and will not be able to make it. She also fears what will happen to her if he dies first.

While money matters are the number-one source of arguments during marriage, calm discussions about money can also be the best way to alleviate such fears. Talking about the plans that are in place for retirement income, including life insurance, can ease her mind. Practical planning and open communication are the keys to alleviating such fears. If she has not been involved in putting the money aside from a weekly or biweekly paycheck, then she is less confident that the money will be there. He needs to have a plan in place and share it with her.

Sitting down and reviewing all possible scenarios with a financial planner (with whom they <u>both</u> feel comfortable) may also be the answer. Knowledge can be very reassuring. If both husband and wife are concerned, or if they started saving for retirement very late in the game, he (or she or both) might consider options for other types of jobs that may be part time but will provide that extra income to make them both breathe easier. In some instances, couples have started businesses together. However, starting a new business is also stressful and may not be the answer if money-related concerns already exist.

SCENARIO #3: **Different Places**

In this situation, the wife, like the husband, has her own career. She may be a few years younger and may have started her career later on or taken some years off when the children were young. Now, however, she's busily fulfilling her goals and career dreams while he's ready to settle down, play golf, travel to exotic places, or simply kick off his shoes and stroll along the beach. Their careers are now at very different places: hers kicking into gear and his winding down.

No, this isn't time to say "See ya." It's time to appreciate each other's individuality while staying together. Of course, this is easier with some advance planning. Unless she's just hitting the workforce while his retirement party is being planned, there will be some overlap in their careers. It is during that time period that they need to talk about the direction they will be taking as a couple when his retirement comes up in three, five, or 10 years.

He needs to plan in advance that he will spend some of his retirement time enjoying the things he wants to do without her, such as hobbies or days on the golf course with his pals. She needs to allow him to enjoy his retirement lifestyle while remaining focused on her goals. He needs to respect her career and what it means to her. He should not expect her to walk away from what is important to her, and she should not expect him to hang around the house or do the chores while waiting until she is also ready to retire.

Many couples find that if they set aside some time to listen to what they are up to in their day-to-day routines and appreciate that each has a lifestyle that makes them happy, they not only continue to feel connected but also take pride in what they are doing. For some couples, particularly those where she has been in the home primarily for many years and he has been working long hours and even traveling out of town on business, it can provide a sense of role reversal. If both husband and wife feel comfortable and secure with their own new roles, they can have some great times and some good laughs about the new direction they've taken. Mutual support and respect are the keys.

SCENARIO #4: You Want to Do What?

They are both retiring and looking forward to their retirement years together. Problem is he wants to spend those years playing golf in Florida, and she wants to spend them being around their family in Wisconsin. If they've neglected to discuss such plans with each other while building up their retirement portfolio, they are in for a rude awakening. The day he strolls in wearing ugly checkered golf pants and carrying photos of potential homes in Del Ray Beach and announces that he's ready to sell their house and move to Florida will be the day he is greeted with a rather surprised "You want to do what!?"

No, you can't be in two places at once. However, you can list the pros and cons of each retirement lifestyle. In the end, however, you'll need to reach a compromise solution. Why do you think there are so many people who spend the winter in Florida and the summer up in the northeast? It's not just about the weather.

Whatever the final decision, it should come with plenty of discussion beginning well in advance. It also may include some trial and error. Don't sell your home. Spend some time renting in Florida and/or Wisconsin (or whichever two places make up the controversy). Whatever lifestyle each party desires, try it out. One of the best aspects of retirement is that unlike work, you're the boss. Therefore, if you don't like one plan, you can essentially quit and try another. The initial two years of retirement allow for such trial and error as long as you leave the major aspects of your life, such as your home and savings, intact.

You may decide that nude volleyball isn't what you thought it would be and perhaps you really would prefer a more traditional retirement lifestyle. If you keep an open mind, you'll be able to make a fair assessment of your partner's choice of retirement lifestyle.

Often, a spouse of 30 or 40 years has a pretty good idea of what his or her partner might really enjoy. "He (or she) was right! I love it here!" is frequently the surprised response from a spouse who tried following his or her partner's retirement dream. Sometimes not. Be flexible.

SCENARIO # 5: It Was Good to Be the King

The phone is always ringing, the secretary holds your calls, and the car is waiting and ready to take you where you want to go. When you speak, like the old E. F. Hutton TV commercials, everyone listens. Well, it may not be that dramatic, but if you have worked your way up to a senior executive position, you are used to commanding a level of respect and having a degree of power that is suddenly gone when you retire. Now, you're answering your own phone—on the rare occasion it rings—and when you walk into a restaurant, you no longer get the preferential treatment. Now you are thinking, "It was good to be king."

Often, individuals who have achieved a high position in business fear that once they retire, their value will diminish. Suddenly, they are not in coveted positions with corner offices. They feel that they are no longer "important."

It can be a tough transition. Where does the former executive go to fill that void? Sometimes this can be very difficult, and days at the country club or being involved in household chores or local activities do not make up the slack.

Sometimes these individuals need to go back into the working world in some capacity. I counsel some former corporate executives to join the board of directors of another corporation. This provides them an opportunity to hold a position of some authority and make key decisions. Others join the ranks of public speaking and share their expertise through seminars and lectures, thus standing up in front of the room and again commanding respect and attention. While it is not easy to replace the level of importance enjoyed by a senior corporate executive, it is possible to utilize the skills and knowledge attained during all of those years of productivity. Teaching can also be very rewarding as a means of passing the torch.

SCENARIO # 6: I Just Wanna Get the "H---" out of Here!

He or she is the person in the office who is crossing off the calendar during the last 365 days to retirement. Each day, the red "x" gets bolder, brighter, bigger. All this person wants to do is get the "H---" out of the office. The employee may be dissatisfied, frustrated, bored, or simply tired of the usual routine. All he or she can think about is how many days until finally retiring. Suddenly, the day arrives. It's like Jack Nicholson in the opening scene of the movie About Schmidt: he is sitting there watching the clock until it hits 5 p.m. The boxes are already packed, and in a flash he is out the door before anyone can even say "good luck."

The problem with this scenario is that retirement is acquainted with running away from something: the job, the boss, the office, or all of the above. Unfortunately, without a retirement plan in place, there is suddenly a large void to fill. Often this type of retiree finds himself or herself, shortly after retirement, feeling frustrated while sitting home and trying to figure out how to restructure life in a meaningful way.

It is important to have both a reason to retire and something to retire to. In some cases, this person needed only a sabbatical or some downtime. In other situations, it wasn't retiring but a change of scenery or a different (perhaps more fulfilling) job that was really needed. Sometimes it has not even been about the job at all but other things in life that make someone decide that such a change is the only answer. Retirement might not have been the best plan of action because it was approached for the wrong reasons.

Unfortunately, too often we make major decisions based on our emotions without a lot of practical planning behind them. It is, therefore, important to take the time to clearly understand why it is that you want to retire and what it is that you want to retire to. Running away or simply getting out of a place in which you don't like working doesn't always make for a fulfilling retirement.

It's also interesting to note that some people who "hated" their jobs actually find that they typically miss them once they retire. They simply didn't realize that there were also aspects of their jobs that they enjoyed, such as the camaraderie, dealing with favorite clients or customers, or even the shared pleasure derived from hating the boss.

SCENARIO # 7: **This Isn't What I Planned**

> *Denise and Fred planned their retirement for several years before he left the company and she retired from her editorial position. They had plans to travel and then settle in a retirement community where they could both enjoy spending time on the golf course. Then, less then two months after the retirement party, Fred had a major heart attack from which he did not recover. All of a sudden, Denise was alone. "This is not what I had planned," she cried.*

Unfortunately, the plans we make may be forced to change along the way. An ongoing illness or the loss of a spouse can change your retirement plans completely. Suddenly, you're retiring alone, and you have to rethink all of those shared plans for the future. "It's so unfair; this isn't what I planned" is the all-too-familiar refrain from someone who has indeed been deprived of the plans he or she made with a partner.

I always try to get my clients not to make major decisions at such an emotional time in life. Working through a loss is a very emotional process, and depending on the individual, it can take a varying degree of time to adjust. Most often, the financial planning for retirement will not change, and the money will still be there, alleviating some of the stress. Time, however, spent doing the smaller and simpler things in life, is usually the best way for someone to begin to put his or her life back together. It's a very rough transitional period.

If a person can surround himself or herself with people close to him or her—be it friends or family—he or she can focus on just getting by for a while and in time moving forward. No, this may not be the retirement lifestyle this person had planned, but sometimes the circumstances are out of anyone's control. Down the road, most people do find happiness with a new plan. The key is not to make major decisions for a while and allow time to heal.

SCENARIO # 8: Who Will Take Care of Me?

When Marcy contemplated retiring, she saw many new adventures in her future—not to mention time to spend with nine grandchildren. At 61 years of age, she retired from teaching elementary school after 36 years. Now, she was primed to move into her retirement lifestyle. Although she had been earning her own way and supporting herself since her divorce some 17 years earlier, she had one major concern. "Who will take care of me as I grow older?" asked Marcy. "I don't want to burden my children, but I'm worried about whether I'll have enough money to cover my expenses should I become ill."

This is a common situation when someone faces retirement alone. He or she has been widowed or divorced for some time now or perhaps was never married. Because the life expectancy of women remains longer than that of men, this is more typically a woman's scenario. *Will I have enough money to support myself? I don't want to end up a bag lady. I'm scared. What if I get ill? Who will take care of me?* These are the very real words of many women who fear the worst, being alone and without financial means.

Men too can find this as a serious emotional concern should they be retiring alone. However, more typically, women relate money to a sense of security while men more often see money as a means of power.

I've discussed this very scenario with many women who are frightened. To these women, as well as men, I stress the importance of long-term care. If there is no spouse in the picture, it is particularly important to be covered, and this might mean part-time work to carry health coverage if they do not still have benefits in place from the company for which they had worked. At 65 years of age, Medicare begins; however, it is important to look at the larger picture and set up a long-term health plan that can even provide some income along the way.

Once a good health plan is in place, many women feel a lot more at ease knowing that money will be there to sustain them should this scenario arise. Then, we work on the social and emotional aspects of retiring alone, which focus heavily on socializing with other people and maintaining an active lifestyle.

■ ■ ■ ■ ■ ■ ■

There are many other potential scenarios that present emotional challenges that need to be addressed while approaching and making the transition into your retirement lifestyle. Retirement itself is a very emotional part of life. Like marriage, it is a transitional period for which you need some time to adjust.

Retirement can also be a time to surround yourself with family and friends while also venturing out and meeting new people. Many retirees have forged close friendships by sharing and discovering new activities. Part of your retirement plan may be to join a club or even hop aboard a "singles cruise." It can be a wonderful time for socializing once you allow yourself to get past the worries and emotions associated with making such a major lifestyle transition.

Retirement may be a ways off, and it is certainly hard to prepare for emotions that you are not yet experiencing. You can, however, be aware that no matter how or where you plan to retire, there may be a strong emotional reaction when the time comes to make the actual transition from working to retirement. As with any major life transition, there may be a flood of memories along with some tears.

When you retire, you may suddenly focus on many of the little things that made up your daily routines, from morning coffee to water cooler chatter to those annoying but necessary office fire drills. Surroundings and friends will suddenly be missed when you go from a career into retirement. In addition, there will be anticipation of what is to come and how well you will adapt to your new lifestyle. As carefully as you can plan for retirement, most people will agree that it will still feel a little strange when you don't get up and head into work the following Monday morning after the big office "send off."

It's Okay!

It's okay to be emotional. Don't try to stifle your feelings. You are just as entitled to them as you are to your retirement package.

You need to allow yourself time to work though your emotions. I always advise people during the transitional time, which can take weeks for some people and months or even a year or two for others, not to make major decisions. Wait until you are beyond the emotional impact of the retirement. Waking up the following Monday morning is not the time to suddenly decide you are selling your house and moving to Florida. Even if you have made your retirement plans, you do not have to jump-start them the first week. Take time to settle into your new lifestyle. Don't make the big decisions at such a critical juncture. There's nothing wrong with starting off slowly with baby steps. Make a calendar and set dates and times when you will do things. Then stick to it. Give yourself some leeway to get adapted to the whole concept of retirement. I tell people not to downsize right away and to give it a year. You may decide you don't really want the big house, or you may decide that the memories are too precious and you don't want to leave. Either way, don't act on your immediate emotional response. Give yourself time.

It should also be mentioned that there may be many more years ahead of you, giving you less reason to make big decisions based on an immediate emotional response to your newfound retirement.

What people fail to take a look at is that we're living a lot longer than previous generations of retirees. People retiring today may reach 85 or 90 years of age. Are they prepared emotionally to think that far ahead? What are they going to do? People need to plan for many years ahead of them. On the other hand, they need to relax for a while first.

Once the transition from working to retirement lifestyle has settled in, it is important emotionally to stay active. Many people get involved in something community based or charitable or give back to the community in some manner. Staying vibrant and being involved keeps people young, and while that is no secret, it is worthy of a reminder.

A Matter of Trust

Another area in which your emotions will come into play is in your selection of a financial advisor to help you through the retirement planning process. Yes, you need to find someone with experience in the field and the right credentials, but you also need to feel good about the person. This is someone in whom you are placing a lot of trust and personal responsibility.

Often, clients will feel somewhat vulnerable with the thought of having no more money coming in once they've retired. They sit down in front of this "stranger" who is supposed to alleviate their fears and help them pave the road to retirement. Naturally, doubts may pop up.

Do I have the right person?

Am I going to be "taken advantage of"?

Is he or she going to do right by me?

Is he or she listening?

Does he or she understand what my fears are?

These are the questions you will ponder as you approach a meeting with a financial advisor. While you cannot protect yourself 100%, you have to go in with your eyes open. It's important to ask a lot of questions. Essentially, you want to interview an advisor as you would a doctor or any other professional with whom you will be working closely.

Find out how long the advisor has been in business and how accessible he or she will be, and ask for references. Call those references, and see what they have to say. Check the local Better Business Bureau, and see whether there are any complaints filed against the advisor. Ask around, and see whether other people you know have worked with this person. Often, the best way to find someone is by word of mouth. This doesn't, however, mean that someone your friend, neighbor, or brother absolutely adored is the right person for you. It's a gut feeling that you need to have that tells you this is someone you want to work with. It's not about the rate of return but about your comfort level.

Over my years in business, I have found that many couples have come to us because the wife was uncomfortable working with a male advisor who talked down to her. It's a gender issue, and sometimes women are more comfortable with a female advisor. In other situations, the advisor is talking down to the couple because they don't meet his or her monetary expectations. Some advisors will work with clients only if they have $500,000 in investable assets. Some will look down their noses at someone if he or she has less than $250,000! Some of the larger firms provide only an 800 number for individuals with less than $100,000 in investable assets.

You don't want to work with an 800 number or with anyone who is condescending. You want a real person ready to work with you. Additionally, you don't want boilerplate service. This is certainly not an industry where one size fits all, so if the advisor tells you that all his or her clients are doing such and such, then he or she is not taking individuality into account. A good advisor wants to hear what you have to say so he or she can tailor a plan to suit your specific needs. He or she should ask about your needs and should take good notes.

He or she should find out from you:

What might happen (positively/negative) that could affect your net worth?

What dangers do you see potentially down the road?

Do you have parents who you may have to support or children who still need your financial help?

How much longer do you see yourself (or yourselves) working?

What do you see yourself doing after you retire?

What is your biggest fear?

If those questions aren't being asked, chances are you're in the wrong place.

Many people come in to meet advisors and have doubts. In my opinion, if the hair on the back of your neck is not lying down and feeling really fuzzy, you may want to go somewhere else. Remember, it's not about rate of return but about finding someone who is going to communicate with you in the good times and bad. Too many advisors talk only about money, but it's about more than that. There are a lot of emotional issues going on when you approach retirement. You need someone who is not praying on the fact that you are emotionally tense and vulnerable but who is instead trying to help you to feel at ease.

Some red flags that you are at the wrong advisor's office:

He or she is immediately trying to sell you something.

He or she does not ask you for a full and detailed background.

He or she talks in generalities about what "all my clients are buying."

He or she is making you feel intimidated or is talking down to you.

He or she has another job and is doing this as a sideline.

He or she isn't willing to educate you or answer your questions but prefers to utter the phrases "Don't worry; I'll handle it" or "Trust me."

Your gut feeling says "Run!"

If any of these are the case, leave and don't look back. This is your retirement, so you need someone who can explain the best options for your personal situation.

In the following chapters, we will look at other factors that will impact your retirement planning. Your emotions will play a role in how you approach factors such as the time horizon for your retirement plan or your risk tolerance, both of which are talked about in Chapter 4.

Get Organized with Knowledge, Discipline and Understanding

3

Once you've made some decisions about your retirement lifestyle, it's time to get serious about how you are going to get there. To do so, you need a starting point, and there's no better place to look for one than by exploring your present situation. By first carefully evaluating your current lifestyle, you can begin looking at the years ahead and what changes will be necessary to create your retirement plan.

Most of us don't have a firm handle on what we're spending today on our current lifestyle. We may have a rough idea but no clear figure in mind. Take a moment to consider what the essentials are costing you right now: food and clothing, heat and home maintenance, utilities, insurance, and property taxes. You can be fairly sure that you'll continue to pay these expenses and that inflation will increase their costs over time. Then look at your other typical expenses. Factor in the little things, including gifts and impulse buys. You might want to select two months out of the year (preferably months without vacations or holidays) and determine exactly how much you spend.

Tracking your weekly or even daily spending is usually a very revealing exercise.

By listing current expenses, you will get an idea of what to look for during your retirement years. Many of the same spending habits will prevail, while others will change depending on your anticipated lifestyle. For example, the money you spend now to commute to and from the office on a daily basis will be less if you have a two-day-a-week part-time job. However, you may be spending more money on a hobby of choice that you have found more time to pursue.

If you know your current spending and savings habits, you can start to determine how they might change in the future.

What Is Your Current Spending Style?

To plan your retirement income needs accurately, you must have some idea of your spending style and how that will translate in your retirement years. Experts frequently comment on three categories of retirement spenders:

1. Those who use their earnings only for living expenses and who try never to use any of the principal, or amount they've invested.

2. Those who plan to spend all their money, both principal and earnings, which is sometimes described as total liquidation.

3. Those who earmark portions of their retirement nest egg for certain expenses, which is also described as selective allocation, or creating mental accounts.

Regardless of your style, you will need to know where and why you spend your money.

At the end of this chapter, I have included a list of possible expenses to help remind you where the money goes. For example, we tend to forget the additional costs involved with having a pet or forget that those five grandchildren are all going to receive gifts on their birthdays. The dollar amounts may or may not be small, but they all add up.

You also need to consider your priorities. What do you envision will be the most important uses of your money in retirement?

Meeting the needs of daily living (food, medical care, housing)?

Having money to do the things you enjoy?

Providing for your heirs?

Making charitable contributions?

If you analyze the way you think about—and subsequently spend—money, you may find that you allocate your assets into distinct categories in your head. You may, for example, put the money you spend on living expenses into one category, what you have set aside for retirement into another, and your investment assets into a third—and you don't mix and match. Then you might *earmark your bonus to pay for a special family vacation*. If you are someone who practices the principle of mental accounting, you wouldn't sell off an investment or borrow the money from a retirement plan to take a vacation but would be comfortable assigning extra income for that use. If handling money that way makes sense to you, you'll be likely to use mental accounting in retirement as well. That can position you to identify which investments you should use for living expenses, which for special expenses, and which for preserving your estate.

Shifting toward Retirement

As you get closer to retirement, you will typically shift assets from higher-risk investments to lower-risk investments. This scenario, however, is not set in stone and will depend on how much money you are talking about, your style of investing, and your expenses. Depending also, in part, on your personality and comfort when it comes to level of risk, you may already be in a "safe" investment mode. In conjunction with shifting your expenditures and investment strategies, you will have to take into account the changes in your sources of income. On top of all of that will be external factors that you have no control over. You can still roughly plan for such potential factors as you go. The bottom line is to start looking at how you will get from point "A," your current financial situation, to point "B," your retirement lifestyle. To do so, you'll have to take into account the positives and negatives that can be anticipated along the way.

As a golfer, I like to use the analogy of teeing off on a 500-yard hole. The flag looks very far away, and you know you can't get there with one swing. You'll need to take several strokes and create a plan to get the ball down the fairway, onto the green, and finally into the cup. You'll be selecting various clubs as you go and trying to work your way around obstacles such as sand traps and water hazards. Life has its share of choices and obstacles that you will also need to work your way through, or around, before reaching your retirement goals. It will be a steady course, and you won't be getting a long "hole in one" unless you win the $37-million lottery—and the odds of that happening are less than getting that long hole in one.

So, now it's time to tee off.

Don't stop at income and expenses. Additional factors you should also consider are your investment portfolio, defined retirement plan, pension, Social Security, life insurance, wills and trusts, health insurance coverage, and so on.

When I meet with people, we look at the household income and assets including savings accounts, money markets, and investments. As mentioned earlier, in trying to determine someone's net worth, I don't like to include home equity because it is not a foregone conclusion that someone wants to sell his or her home. Nor should it be presumed that the next place of residence will necessarily be less expensive.

Naturally, your plans will change over time. However, having a plan, no matter how tentative, is better than not having one at all. It's akin to having a road map on a journey. It may not be easy to follow, and you still might veer off course, but it's better than having no map and no idea which direction to take.

To determine your net worth, evaluate your current assets. Your net worth includes the value of your:

- Savings accounts

- Investments such as stocks, bonds, and mutual funds

- Money market funds

- CDs

- Cash value life insurance

- Pension plan

- Employer-sponsored savings plans (i.e., 401(k) and 403(b))

- Business interests

- Traditional or Roth IRAs

- Self-employed plans such as simplified employee pensions (SEP) and Keogh plans

- Cash

- Other real estate (not including your home, which as mentioned earlier you should not factor into the equation)

Taken together, these values should make up your total assets.

To determine your net worth, from this total dollar figure, you need to subtract your liabilities:

- Mortgage(s)

- Home equity loans

- Personal loans

- Credit card debt

- Auto loans

- Any other debts or ongoing payments for which you are responsible

The difference between your assets and liabilities is your net worth.

That is your starting point. From there, once you determine your choice of retirement lifestyle or have a fairly good idea of what that lifestyle should be, you can begin to look at where you will need to be at the time of your retirement.

Along with putting together your current and anticipated list of expenses, you should try to determine which expenses are likely to go up and which are likely to go down.

Here's a starting point. You can fill in the rest.

Costs that could go down:		Costs that could go up:	
Home mortgage	_____	Health care	_____
Commuting	_____	Travel	_____
Financial responsibility for children	_____	Second home	_____
Hobbies	_____	Financial responsibility for parents	_____
Work-related clothing	_____		

In the past, retirement experts generally agreed that you would need between 70% and 80% of your preretirement income to maintain your standard of living after you stop working. Today, with the effects of inflation, a longer average life span, and more active retirement lifestyles, this formula may be too simplistic. You may need as much as 90% or even 100% of your current income during your retirement years, especially as you make the initial transition.

It is also important that you factor in all the emotionally driven "costs" associated with retiring, such as leaving a legacy to children and grandchildren or a large endowment to a favorite charity or university, world travels, or shooting under 80 for 18 holes of golf (all those lessons). These need to be factored into your retirement income requirements.

Therefore, you should make a comparable list of anticipated expenses and costs for your retirement years. Naturally, some costs will remain the same as they are presently, such as basic necessities. However, your change in lifestyle will dictate where more or less money will go. Follow your goals, and include the areas that will matter most.

It is possible that mortgage payments will likely no longer need to be included. Don't be so quick, however, to eliminate other areas such as car payments. Even though your current automobile may be fully paid off, it is unlikely that it will last you another 10, 15, or 20 years. You will likely be purchasing another vehicle during your retirement years. While you might be trading in a family-sized SUV for a more practical smaller car, you will still incur some additional expense.

Plan on the basis of practical and realistic dreams and goals. You need not try to "cut corners." On the other hand, you most likely won't be enjoying the lifestyle of Donald Trump or Bill Gates. Few people do.

Tax and Inflation Planning

Sorry to interrupt your pleasant retirement dreams with subjects like taxes and inflation, but they will, unfortunately, be part of the equation.

Tax planning is essential to preserving the strength of your retirement income- generating programs. Whether you are a victim of the tax system or use it to your advantage, there can be no wealth accumulation without a sound tax strategy. The right strategies can increase the effectiveness of your savings and investments dramatically without any additional outlay of funds.

Over time, tax laws are modified to reflect changes in the economy, shifts in political thinking, and the ever-evolving attitudes toward investing. For example, the penalty for excess withdrawals from IRAs and other retirement plans was dropped in recent years, the ceiling on contributions to other plans was raised, the amount of money that could be "gifted" to heirs tax free increased, and in 1998, the Roth IRA came into existence. Sometimes existing rules are grandfathered, meaning they continue to apply to existing plans but not to new ones. Many tax changes continue to occur, and you will need to shift your strategies as the tax laws are amended. For now, however, you can take advantage of the existing opportunities to build your retirement assets and hope for the best.

Taxes and Social Security

Planning would not be complete without the consideration of income taxes. A common comment from clients when they first come to my office is "We will be in a lower income tax bracket at retirement." Many retirees do not even consider the effect of taxes on their income and consider even less so the possible effect of taxes on their Social Security. Fortunately, or unfortunately, depending on how you look at it, most retirees are in the same or close to the same tax bracket at retirement as they were when they worked.

The income tax effect is necessary to review for two reasons. First, when determining how much you will need to maintain your lifestyle, we need to "gross up" your monthly income needs to include income taxes. If you need $40,000 to cover your annual expenses, then we need to determine how much of that $40,000 is going to be taxable and then increase the $40,000 by the taxes due.

The unknown here is how income tax brackets will change over time. Generally, when I ask people where they think taxes are going—up or down— they say up. That being the case, by using today's tax laws, we could be undercalculating the need in later years. Again, this is another reason for the constant monitoring of your situation. If and/or when tax laws change, these changes must be factored into the equation.

Second, a person's gross income can cause his or her Social Security income to be taxed. The rules are different for retirees under normal retirement age (under age 65) and those at normal retirement age (which is gradually increasing from 65 to 67).

In 2005, if a person is under normal retirement age for the whole year and earns more than $11,640, $1 of benefit will ordinarily be lost for each $2 of earnings over $11,640. The annual exempt amount will be increased each year as wage levels rise. Adjustments apply to the exemption if a person reaches normal retirement during the year.

If the retiree is the normal retirement age or older, no benefits are lost because of his or her earnings.

Additionally, federal income tax is applied to the retirees whose income exceeds certain levels. If the total of a person's income plus half of his or her benefits is more than the base amount (listed below), some of the benefits are taxable. Included in the person's total income is any tax-exempt interest income, excludable interest from U.S. savings bonds, and excludable income earned in a foreign country, U.S. possession, or Puerto Rico. This income accessment is called your "provisional income." Depending on a person's provisional income, he or she may be required to include either 50% or 85% of benefits in income.

The base amounts are as follows:

Single Return Filers

- If provisional income is between $25,000 and $34,000
  - Up to 50% Taxed

- If provisional income is above $34,000
  - Up to 85% Taxed

Joint Return Filers

- If provisional income is between $32,000 and $44,000
  - Up to 50% Taxed

- If provisional income is above $44,000
  - Up to 85% Taxed

As written in the Social Security manual by the National Underwriter Company, "Non-taxable interest income is included in income to limit opportunities for manipulation of tax liability on benefits."

You can see how all this fits together for planning purposes. You may be using municipal bonds in your portfolio to decrease your taxable income, but at the same time, you are affecting the taxation on your Social Security benefits. Also, given our graduated income tax scale, it is important to understand where you stand on that scale and how income from investments can put you in a higher bracket. Remember, it is not what you make but what you keep.

This is why we stress the fact that you must not look at any one part of your planning in a vacuum. All the pieces fit together.

Planning for Inflation's Bite

The impact of long-term inflation on purchasing power means that returns must stay ahead of the rate of inflation. This is especially true because of the increase in life expectancy. As inflation continues to rise, sometimes at an unsteady rate, you'll need to keep pace with your income needs. In addition, health care inflation raises the stakes far higher because historically it has increased at two to three times the general inflation rate. Today, with many people paying more for health care and seeing less coverage from existing plans, this becomes a key factor in the quest to stay ahead of the rate of inflation.

Here's a powerful example. Many people think that fixed accounts are safe investments, but if you consider that, on average, a fixed account earns 2.5% after tax and inflation averages 2.9%, clearly, fixed-account investing is not a break-even situation. Thus, you have an investment that may be "safe" but one that is virtually guaranteed to lose money over time. Offsetting the erosion from inflation is a key component of planning. It doesn't mean that you do not have the safe fixed-income investments, but it does mean that you should diversify and maintain a certain percentage of your assets in investments that are likely to outpace inflation and taxes.

The bottom line: your money needs to be invested aggressively enough to produce a worthwhile return after inflation.

■ ■ ■ ■ ■ ■ ■

Spending More!?

You may not believe it at first, but it is very likely that during the first two years of retirement, you may be spending more money than you do now. Often, people shake their heads in disbelief. However, I've seen numerous examples of couples and singles who leave the workforce and shift into their retirement lifestyle with many new activities and plans on their "to do" lists.

Those 40-hour workweeks may have limited your ability to go out and spend money enjoying your hobbies, spoiling your grandchildren, updating your home, and doing all the things you've wanted to do. As it turns out, there are plenty of ways to spend money when you have the added time to go out and enjoy hobbies, grandchildren, and even new business ventures.

There's no need to panic. Simply plan for a little "retirement spending spree" for the first year or two before you settle into a more balanced lifestyle. With proper planning, the money will be there for you to enjoy.

■ ■ ■ ■ ■ ■ ■

Your Retirement Income Program

Now that you've listed your expenses, you'll have to start focusing on your likely sources of income during the retirement years.

Investment dividends, savings and pension plans, Social Security, and any income you'll have from full- or part-time work in retirement will all be included.

While these areas will be discussed in greater detail later in the book, it is very important to start thinking about the potential income sources that will be available to you during your retirement years.

Today's retirees are looking more closely at their own personal savings plans and investments rather than relying on the government and Social Security. Many are considering jobs or even new careers. Some are planning to start their own business enterprises. However, with a new business, it is unwise to factor profits into income until actually setting sail on such a new adventure. Most new businesses do not make money in their first year or two.

In the past, Social Security comprised up to a third or more of a retiree's income, and a company pension plan might provide perhaps another 25% to 30%, with personal savings and investments providing the balance. In more recent years, these percentages have shifted, and the responsibility for building retirement income has been transferred to the individual. Company pension plans, which pay retirement benefits on the basis of salary and years of service, are less commonly found today. They have given way to the rise of defined-contribution plans such as the 401(k) and 403(b). The growth of these retirement plans is in response to the widening gap between Social Security and the cost of living. Social Security was never intended as a full means of support during the retirement years, and today it does not even stretch as far as it once did. Many pension plans are also unable to keep pace with the rate of inflation. Add to that the number of companies that have filed for bankruptcy in recent years (or packed up and shut down completely) and it is clear why the onus of responsibility has changed and placed retirement planning into the hands of the individual.

The modern-day employee typically makes pretax contributions to these plans through payroll deduction up to allowable limits each year. Some of these programs include employer-matching contributions; some do not. The employee directs the investments in these plans and is fully responsible for the monitoring of those investments and the resulting total value of the account. It might be noted that the majority of people investing in retirement plans take little time to ever look over their investments after making the initial decision. They continue contributing directly through their paychecks but do not take a hands-on approach to managing their 401(k) or 403(b). Not that significant adjustments need to be made often, but everyone should keep tabs on how and where the money is invested.

Although the state of the market in recent years has caused many employees great concern about how much remains in such defined-contribution plans, these plans are still a solid part of a retirement portfolio.

In the future, retirees will have to use an even greater percentage of their own funds to pay for many of their expenses in retirement. That's going to require sound planning.

You can't just arrive on retirement's doorstep with a rough idea of what you have and what you'll need to enjoy the lifestyle you have in mind.

The Keys to a Solid Retirement Income Program

You need to plan carefully when setting up a solid retirement income program. Like a good chef, you'll need to mix the right ingredients.

Such ingredients include:

- Knowledge

- Disciplined and consistent savings and investing

- A clear vision of your retirement lifestyle

- Time

■ Knowledge

Ignorance may be bliss but not when it comes to retirement planning.

One of the primary reasons many people don't plan is that they don't think they need to. They don't focus on how Social Security is a diminishing factor in their overall retirement plan. They go through their working years thinking it's all taken care of because they have a pension and Social Security.

It is important to become knowledgeable about the ever-changing economy and the need to take matters of financing a retirement into your own hands.

You need to understand the different sources of retirement income and how they work together to create a total program of income. Consider the following questions:

- How should your personal savings and investments be managed to produce the levels of return that will support the retirement lifestyle you want?

- How do you build an investment portfolio that will provide the income you'll need?

- Which of the investment categories available to you are you comfortable using?

- What is your investment risk tolerance?

- Why is it risky to be too heavily invested in fixed-income investments such as bonds or CDs?

- Can your investment choices outpace inflation?

- How confident do you feel about making financial decisions?

Answers to many of these questions will be found as you read the remaining chapters.

The opportunities to invest for your long-term needs continue to expand. The past decade has opened up more investment opportunities then ever before with a wide variety of mutual funds, stocks, bonds, and other options to choose from. There are investment opportunities for different levels of risk and those that pay steady income. You need to learn about the various options and begin to look at the long-term picture with a knowledge of what different types of investments can do for you. This is an area where a financial advisor can be very beneficial in explaining the various options.

■ Disciplined and consistent savings and investing

Remember: slow but steady still wins the race.

Let's face it. You're not going to lose weight unless you diet and exercise regularly. Fads simply don't work. Likewise, you're not going to have money tucked away for your retirement lifestyle unless you save and invest money on a consistent basis. By saving money, I mean simply not spending it. Americans tend to spend more than they should, saving at an average of less than 5% of their gross annual income. As a rule of thumb, you should save 10% to 15% of your gross annual income in savings plans and investments, with anywhere from 40% to 80% of those assets invested for growth, depending on your age and risk tolerance. (More on risk tolerance later.)

Making regular contributions to your investment vehicle(s) of choice is the only way in which you will succeed at putting money away for retirement. Just as 401(k) and 403(b) plans have money taken directly out of your paycheck and invested for you, you need to do the same thing for yourself. Defined-contribution plans are usually not enough. It's up to you to "pay yourself first" and set aside x amount of dollars on a regular basis before paying anything else. This method of regularly contributing to your own retirement plan will have you using the old dollar cost averaging method of investing.

Dollar cost averaging involves continuous investment in securities, regardless of fluctuating price levels. You need to consider your ability to continue purchases through periods of low price levels or changing economic conditions. Such a plan does not assure a profit, nor does it protect against a loss in a declining market. However, it is an easy way to implement diversification in your investment program. This means that you are buying securities at regular intervals with a fixed dollar amount. Under this system, you buy based on the dollars rather than the number of shares. If each investment is the same number of dollars (for example, $250 from every paycheck), payments buy more shares when the price is low and fewer when it rises. Thus, you make purchases in both good times and bad, and the price at which the shares are eventually sold is more than their average cost. Dollar cost averaging also takes emotion out of the investment process. This means you don't stop and mull over whether it is the right time to invest. The reality is that it is always a good time to invest in your own retirement because the various markets traditionally even out over time. Using this method makes you systematic, disciplined, and focused on the long term. The short-term highs and lows won't bother you because you'll be working with long-term averages and slow overall rises in your portfolio value.

Diversification is also a key component of investing. The term "diversification" refers to investing in a variety of assets—stocks, bonds, real estate, etc.—in order to lower portfolio risk. Although diversifying will not guarantee greater returns or protection against the risk of loss in a declining market, it will reduce volatility if proper diversification methodology is utilized. And you can also diversify across time by investing monthly using dollar cost averaging discussed above. When you do so, you invest at market peaks and valleys, evening out your overall investments. You limit the purchases you make during market highs and ensure that you're sometimes buying at market lows.

■ A clear vision of your retirement lifestyle

Unless you know where you are going, you'll never know when you've arrived.

As discussed earlier and reiterated throughout the rest of this book, it is important to have a mental picture of your retirement lifestyle—one that is both realistic and enjoyable for you. This will require discussion with your spouse because your lifestyle choices for retirement may differ, but in the end, you need to have that Norman Rockwell painting of the two of you in your retirement years etched in your mind, whether it's moving to a new location, traveling abroad, spending time at home with hobbies and grandchildren, or starting a new career.

Yes, external factors may change, and you may need to paint new brush strokes over the original plans, but you need to start working your way toward a goal, and the more planning you have in place, the easier it is to reach that goal or adjust to the changes that take place along the way.

■ Time

In the words of the Rolling Stones, "Time is on your side—yes, it is."

Time is your greatest asset. Your ability to create the retirement of your dreams depends more on this single factor than on anything else. If you start planning at 40, you'll be in a far better position than if you start at 50, even if you have half the resources of a 50-year-old.

Time lets you make midcourse corrections in your plan and adjust to external factors that may occur between now and the time you retire from your regular work schedule. It also lets you take advantage of one of the great mysteries of the universe: compounding. Compounding essentially means that your money is earning money. Without getting into detail, it works on the basis of interest growing on interest. In other words, once you receive interest on the original amount you have invested, the next time you receive interest, it will be on the larger amount (your original investment plus the first interest added).

What this means is that the first dollar you invest is the most powerful because it has the most time to experience the effects of compounding. It also means that the earlier you start, the less you need to set aside and the more you will have in the end. The difference of even just a few percentage points can amount to hundreds or thousands of dollars in total returns over the long term.

In this chapter, we have focused on many of the practical aspects of planning for your retirement. While listing expenses and income is a "practical" exercise, in the next chapter, we will start looking at identifying your risk tolerance, time horizon, and some potential obstacles that may stand in your way of achieving your goals. These will not show up on your budget but will help shape and mold the decisions that you make along the way. Retirement is a major adjustment in your life. While you can have all of the dollar signs in place, it is more important that you feel good about the picture in front of you and understand where you are headed. After all, it's your picture of retirement.

EXPENSES

Expenses: (Separated into those expenses that are Mandatory and those that are Discretionary)

1. Fixed — Mandatory Expenses

Loans	MONTHLY	ANNUALLY
Home Mortgage (Residence)		
Home Improvement		
Auto(s)		
School		
Other		
TOTAL LOANS		

Insurance		
Life (All Policies)		
Disability (All Policies)		
Medical (All Policies)		
Homeowners/Renters		
Personal Property Floaters		
Auto		
Other		
TOTAL INSURANCE		

Taxes		
Real Estate Tax (Residence)		
Real Estate Tax (Other)		
Federal Income Tax		
State Income Tax		
Local Income Tax		
FICA		
Other		
TOTAL TAXES		

Other Payroll Deductions   MONTHLY   ANNUALLY

Credit Union

Pension

State Unemployment

Disability

Other

TOTAL OTHER PAYROLL DEDUCTIONS

Services

Water and Sewer

Garbage Collection

Other

TOTAL SERVICES

Miscellaneous

Education (Tuition, etc.)

Rent

Alimony/Child Support

Union Dues

Other

TOTAL MISCELLANEOUS

Total Fixed — Mandatory Expenses

2. Variable — Mandatory Expenses

Necessities	MONTHLY	ANNUALLY
Food and other Grocery Items	_____	_____
Medical and Dental (Nonreimbursed)	_____	_____
Drugs (Nonreimbursed)	_____	_____
Clothing	_____	_____
Child Care	_____	_____
Other	_____	_____
TOTAL NECESSITIES	_____	_____

Utilities		
Electricity	_____	_____
Natural Gas	_____	_____
Heating Oil	_____	_____
Telephone	_____	_____
Other	_____	_____
TOTAL UTILITIES	_____	_____

Transportation		
Auto Fuel	_____	_____
Auto Maintenance and Repairs	_____	_____
Auto Tags and Drivers Licenses	_____	_____
Public Transportation (Taxis, Buses)	_____	_____
TOTAL TRANSPORTATION	_____	_____

Total Variable — Mandatory Expenses	_____	_____

3. Variable — Discretionary Expenses

Home   MONTHLY   ANNUALLY

    Maintenance   _____   _____

    Improvements   _____   _____

    Furnishings   _____   _____

    Maintenance Pool/Tennis Court, etc. _____   _____

    Other   _____   _____

    TOTAL HOME   _____   _____

Recreation

    Entertainment: Movies/Plays   _____   _____

    Vacation/Travel   _____   _____

    Athletic Activities   _____   _____

    Restaurants   _____   _____

    Baby-Sitters   _____   _____

    TOTAL RECREATION   _____   _____

Animals

    Licenses   _____   _____

    Food   _____   _____

    Veterinarian   _____   _____

    Other   _____   _____

    TOTAL ANIMALS   _____   _____

Publications

    Magazines   _____   _____

    Newspapers   _____   _____

    Books   _____   _____

    Music and CDs   _____   _____

    Other   _____   _____

    TOTAL PUBLICATIONS   _____   _____

Personal Care	MONTHLY	ANNUALLY
Hair Care	_____	_____
Outside Laundry/Dry Cleaning	_____	_____
Toiletries/Cosmetics	_____	_____
Other	_____	_____
TOTAL PERSONAL CARE	_____	_____

Miscellaneous		
Gifts	_____	_____
Allowances	_____	_____
Lessons (Dance, etc.)	_____	_____
Contributions	_____	_____
Care of Elderly Relative	_____	_____
Unreimbursed Expenses	_____	_____
Nonfood Items	_____	_____
Other	_____	_____
TOTAL MISCELLANEOUS	_____	_____

Savings/Investments		
KEOGH	H _____	W _____
IRA	H _____	W _____
TOTAL SAVINGS/INVESTMENTS	_____	_____

	MONTHLY	ANNUALLY
1. Fixed — Mandatory Expenses	_____	_____
2. Variable — Mandatory Expenses	_____	_____
3. Variable — Discretionary Expenses	_____	_____
TOTAL EXPENSES	_____	_____

4 Considering the Big Picture on Risk

As you approach the retirement planning process, there are several key areas on which you will need to focus, including your **time horizon** (how long before you retire), level of **risk tolerance**, and the **potential obstacles** that may stand in the way of reaching your retirement goals. In this section, I'll discuss how each of these important factors will affect your specific retirement plan. In each case, your personal situation needs to be considered. Remember, there are no boilerplate retirement plans.

Time Horizon

There are actually two areas to look at when discussing your time horizon in regard to retirement planning. First, there is the amount of time you have until you retire. This is the time frame you have to establish your retirement plan and put it into action. How many years are you away from retirement? That number will influence your plan significantly. The more years until retirement, the more options you may have for building up your portfolio and making appropriate adjustments along the way.

The second part of your time horizon is the estimated longevity of you and your spouse. While no one knows for sure what his or her life expectancy will be, there are people today living well into their 90s and even reaching 100 and beyond. Therefore, if you are eligible for an early retirement at the age of 50, you could have nearly 50 more years ahead of you. If, however, you want to keep on working until 65 or even 70, you will be planning for 20 or possibly even 30 years of retirement income. Either way, there are a number of years in which you will be receiving income from the retirement plan you set up today.

Years to Retirement

Although the concept of retirement has changed dramatically over the past 20 years, for most people, there is typically a time when they begin looking forward to calling it quits and moving on to other aspects of life, be it relaxation or starting a business.

Although you may change your mind, you will typically set a target date for such a change of plans. If, for example, you are age 50 and have decided that at 62 you'd like to call it a career at your corporate position and take on a new adventure, you then have 12 years in which to prepare your finances for retirement from that phase of your life.

Most people who I see come to me in their late 40s or early 50s—some even later on. Sure, they have been contributing to their 401(k) plans since they were 30, but until now, they have not really thought about their impending retirement lifestyle. And why should they? There's no reason to be thinking of retirement when you're 32 and busily trying to figure out how you'll save up enough money for your six-year-old son's college tuition. Juggling the payments for a new car and a mortgage leaves most people little time to stop and consider retirement funding. However, once the kids get older and they begin thinking of other options they might enjoy pursuing, they'll likely begin focusing more attention on retirement planning.

I look for the best means of building a portfolio based on the time factor involved in conjunction with each individual's risk tolerance factor. For your money to work for you, during this time period, you have to get it "gainfully employed" in the right investment vehicles.

Typically, the closer you are to retirement, the more conservative you will want to be with your investment portfolio because there is less time to make up for any losses or downturns in the market. However, with life expectancy being what it is today, we also need to consider that you may need to generate income for a long period of time, perhaps 40 more years. Therefore, we don't want to get too conservative. Don't forget we also have to outpace inflation over that time as well as factor in taxes.

Longevity

The second part of time horizon, as noted above, takes that very issue—longevity—into account. We'd all like to be George Burns or Eubie Blake and keep on living a good life until the age of 100. If your parents enjoyed longevity and you lead a relatively healthy lifestyle, you may also enjoy your ninetieth, ninety-fifth, or one-hundredth birthday, or even more.

I discuss family longevity, lifestyle, and other factors in an effort to estimate how long an individual may be enjoying his or her retirement years. Certainly, the younger someone retires, the more emphasis that must be put on balancing growth (necessary to outpace inflation and taxes) and income. Here too we will look at a portfolio that addresses the post retirement time horizon.

A young retiree may plan to work elsewhere for 10 or more years, and that too needs to be considered. If he or she continues earning an income, then we might opt to be more aggressive for a longer amount of time because the need for income from investment vehicles may not be significant for several more years. There are numerous potential scenarios, and it's important to consider them all realistically. It is also important to prepare for unexpected obstacles that may occur.

The first chart represents the outcome of investing with a various mix of stocks and bonds.

Asset Mix

	Aggressive	Growth	Balanced	Conservative
Stocks	80%	60%	40%	15%
Bonds	20%	40%	60%	85%

The two charts included here illustrate the difference in planning when approaching retirement. The first chart looks at years to retirement while accumulating assets. The second looks at distribution of assets during retirement.

Chart 1

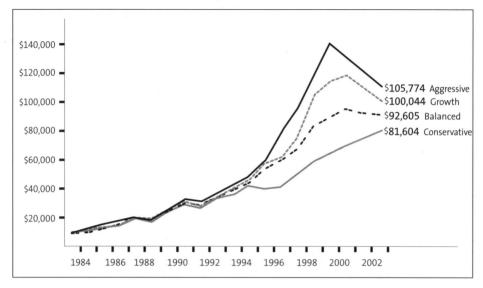

Sources: Standard & Poor's; Federal Reserve, 2002. Stocks are represented by the S&P 500, an unmanaged index that is generally considered representative of the U.S. stock market. Bonds are represented by long-term Treasuries (10+ years maturity) and constructed from yields published by the Federal Reserve. Illustration is for the 20-year period ending December, 2002. Investors cannot invest directly in any index. Portfolio allocations are hypothetical and are not based on any particular product or investment. Past pe rformance does not guarantee future results.

Stocks Can Also help you avoid running out of money during retirement

Conventional wisdom tells you that it's prudent to invest conservatively during retirement to make your money last. But actually, the reverse is true. Once you have retired, you may need to include stocks in your portfolio to protect against outliving your assets. To plan correctly, you'll need to decide how much income you can safely withdraw from your retirement portfolio without running the risk of depleting your assets prematurely. Financial consultants utilize a statistical method called the Monte Carlo simulation to help their clients manage this decision. With a Monte Carlo simulation, thousands of random outcomes are generated as a way of determining probability. Eventually, a pattern emerges showing the most likely scenarios to occur.

The accompanying table, built from a Monte Carlo simulation, gives you an idea of how different withdrawal rates will increase the likelihood that you will run out of money. For example, the table suggests there is a 90% chance that a mix of 40% stocks and 60% bonds will not sustain a 6% withdrawal rate, adjusted for inflation, for a 30-year retirement. On the basis of tables like this, financial consultants generally recommend a balanced portfolio and a withdrawal rate of no more than 4% to 5%.

Likelihood you will not sustain a 30-year retirement
Chart 2

STOCK/BOND ALLOCATION

	100/0	80/20	60/40	40/60	15/85	5/95
4%	15%	12%	14%	15%	29%	63%
5%	32%	34%	42%	58%	91%	100%
6%	53%	59%	72%	90%	100%	100%
7%	76%	82%	93%	99%	100%	100%

<< Less Likely   More Likely >>

Risk Tolerance

One of the many questions I ask clients is, *What does money mean to you?* As discussed earlier, for women, I've found that it often means safety or security, while for men, it means power (although they don't phrase it in that way) and, ultimately, the freedom to do whatever they want. Typically, women are more conservative and men are more aggressive by nature, and this holds true when determining risk tolerance as it relates to investing. Although this is a broad generality, it is very often the case between husbands and wives.

Janet and Tom Jacobson are the perfect example of being far afield on their risk tolerance toward investing. Their answers on the risk tolerance questionnaire indicated clearly that Tom wanted to take risks in every aspect of life including having his own business and that Janet, a homemaker, was always concerned that they would run out of money. There was enough risk in the business that she didn't want to take any additional risk in how their money was being managed. What we had to do was come up with a manner in which he would feel "in control" and would be able to gain more wealth by taking greater risks. She needed to have a sense of security, knowing that there would be money available to them for their retirement needs. She had her own assets, and we literally divided up all of their assets into separate accounts so they could satisfy their own levels of risk.

This approach is great for helping clients maintain their risk tolerance in a portion of their assets while taking into consideration what their long-term needs will be. In some cases, the wife may need to take on a little bit more risk in order to achieve those goals. Sometimes we need to go through an educational process to help these women feel comfortable and slowly over time invest in the market and take on an additional risk as their comfort level warrants.

The bottom line is that some people are more willing to roll the dice and take risks while others like to play it closer to the vest and opt for the conservative approach.

Your temperament and personality have evolved in such ways that you either have a strong tolerance for risk or you don't. Perhaps you've been burned by bad investments in the past. Maybe you were brought up with an understanding of the need to hold onto your money closely. Or, maybe you've always enjoyed a little taste of adventure and have been known to throw caution to the wind, so to speak. No matter how you've reached your current level of risk tolerance, it will factor heavily into how you plan your retirement portfolio from an emotional standpoint.

Alternatives need to be discussed when emotionally a couple is unwilling to take on more risk in order to achieve their goals. Working longer or lowering expenses are both options that are sometimes critical to the planning process. It's better to determine this before retiring. Any investment counselor should assess how much risk a client is comfortable taking and then work within those parameters when trying to advise him or her.

The basic principle behind risk when investing is that the more risk you take, the higher the potential rewards. Also, the greater the risk, the greater the volatility! The other side of the coin is taking the low-risk approach. Taking less risk usually means that the return on your investment will be less but your investment is safer. An example of a higher-risk investment would be a sector mutual fund like technology, which has great volatility. A low-risk investment would be a money market fund or a fixed-income mutual fund.

Typically, the more time you have before reaching your impending goal—which in this case is retirement—the more risk you can take. Traditionally, the stock market, over time, has always proven to recover from downturns, and if you invest in the market with a long-term approach, you will make money.

While any investment will have some risk attached, the key to building your retirement portfolio will be to balance higher- and lower-risk investments in a manner that:

- Will meet your goals and retirement needs

- Allows you to feel comfortable from a risk tolerance perspective (you can sleep at night)

- Outpaces inflation and other factors that can eat away at your potential nest egg

Below I have included a risk tolerance questionnaire. Take the test to evaluate where you stand. Any investment advisor should offer a similar test and act accordingly. If your advisor disregards your level of risk and tries to push investment products that will give you sleepless nights, then you are not working with the right advisor.

A portfolio should balance out your level of risk by diversifying between various investment vehicles. You may, for example, have a 50-50 split between high-risk investments and low-risk investments. For the sake of comfort, or a lower tolerance for risk, you may opt for 35% high-risk investments and 65% low-risk investments. The choice should be based on guidance from your advisor in conjunction with your comfort level or tolerance for risk and both time horizons as discussed above. The idea is to put together a mixed portfolio that meets your needs. If, for example, we factor everything into account, including inflation, and come back with a 6% rate of return but the retirement lifestyle you're seeking would need an 8% rate of return, you would have to either reduce your expectations or increase your risk.

Over the years, I have found that people who are greater risk takers as investors are also more likely to spend their money more freely. On the other hand, people who are conservative with their investments are also more conservative spenders. Typically, this works out well because more conservative investments will generate a lower rate of return, leaving the conservative spender with less money to spend anyway. I can't recall meeting someone who wanted to invest conservatively but was aggressive when it came to spending money.

Potential Obstacles

Potential obstacles are those issues that come up and drain away some of the funds earmarked for retirement. Taxes and inflation are two obstacles that you cannot totally avoid. We will generally factor a 3% inflation rate when preparing retirement calculations. However, it is not something that we can accurately predict. Most recently, inflation has been very low, but if you recall, in the early 1980s, we hit double-digit numbers.

The greatest potential obstacle most retirees face is whether one or both parties will need to be in some type of assisted-care facility. The question is whether they will have enough funds to support that additional cost. In some cases, there may be enough funds for one person but not enough for the surviving spouse.

Health care today is a significant concern for my clients and anyone approaching retirement. The costs are increasing, and Medicare does not help significantly; it only serves as a supplement to reduce some of the expenses. Many of my clients are leaving major corporations where they receive ongoing health benefits. There are, however, significant concerns and questions, such as:

1. What can individuals do who are leaving companies that do not provide such health care?

2. What happens if the company can no longer provide the health care package?

3. What if the health care provided does not cover the needs of the spouse?

The ever-changing laws and the tenuous state of many companies leave soon-to-be retirees less than comfortable about their impending health care status. Therefore, this is an area we try to cover carefully while structuring a plan. Where will the money for health care, especially long-term care, come from? If there is any risk of losing those benefits, we incorporate the potential cost of health insurance in the budget so we are prepared.

Supporting Family Members

Another obstacle that has become increasingly more common has been that of supporting either parents or children. Increased life expectancy has made it more possible to retire at the age of 55 and be helping to support your mother or father who is in his or her late 70s, 80s, or 90s. This is an additional expense that you need to allocate for when planning your own retirement, particularly because many seniors did not have the savings mechanisms available 25 or 30 years ago when they planned for their own retirement needs.

The past 20 years have seen the average age of persons marrying slowly rise. Two careers, graduate school, and in some cases prior marriages have created family planning at a slightly later stage of life than in previous generations. Couples close to the age of 40 are more commonly having children, and in many cases, the new father is over 40. Therefore, it is not uncommon for a 62-year-old retiree to be supporting, or helping to support, his 19- or 20-year-old son or daughter while he or she attends college or embarks on postcollege life. This too precipitates a need for additional income.

To try to best accommodate the situation, you should first look at your own retirement situation without these additional costs. Next, look at the additional costs separately and determine whether you can handle them and what concessions you may need to make to do so. If you determine that you will need to pay an additional $30,000 a year for a nursing home for a parent or toward college tuition for your child, you'll need to look at how to alter your plans. This might mean downsizing or taking on a part-time job to supplement your income. You can also work to adjust your portfolio, but this may mean having to take on greater risk to cover the additional expenses. Alternatively, you may research state nursing homes or local college alternatives or scholarships. These decisions are often very emotional and need to be made with your heart, as well as with your financial advisor.

When Bill and Anita Johnson came to see me, he was 65 and retired, and she was 57 and did not work. Bill's mother was in private nursing home, and it was costing them approximately $40,000 a year. It was quite evident, based on their lifestyle, that if they continued paying the $40,000 a year for the nursing home, it would be impossible for them to maintain their retirement goals. Because of health reasons, Bill could not go back to work, and Anita had not worked in many years. It was, therefore, a very tough and very emotional decision, but they would have to consider putting his mother into a state-run facility where the state would pick up most of the cost and they would supplement as best they could. They spent a lot of time doing research and finally found a state nursing facility that was near their home. They were able to oversee the care that was provided to his mother while not destroying the retirement plan that we had created for them.

Knowing your parents' financial situation is often critical to maintaining your lifestyle in retirement and can alleviate some very tough and emotional decisions such as in the case of Bill and Anita.

Once you have determined your own level of risk tolerance, calculated how many years you have until retirement, and explored potential obstacles that may arise, you can begin looking at the ways and means in which you can establish, monitor, and build your retirement portfolio. In the next chapter, we will explore the various means of income that you will have available to you in your retirement years and how you can formulate a system that allows for your money to grow while providing you with the steady income you will need to cover your expenses.

Risk Tolerance Questionnaire

The profile below will help determine your overall risk tolerance and can guide you and your advisors in developing an overall personal investment profile and policy. Please remember: there are no right or wrong answers.

1. **My current age is:**

   a. Less than 45 years

   b. 45–55 years

   c. 56–65 years

   d. 66–75 years

   e. More than 75 years

2. **In how many years do you plan to retire?**

   a. More than 16 years

   b. 13–15 years

   c. 8–12 years

   d. 4–7 years

   e. 3 years or less

3. **When thinking about your retirement savings, where would you place yourself on the following scale?**

   a. I want my money to have as much growth potential as possible, regardless of fluctuation in account value.

   b. I want to maintain a balanced mix of investments with some fluctuation in account value.

   c. I want as much assurance as possible that the value of my retirement savings will not go down.

4. **Which of the following best describes your attitude about long-term investing in income securities (such as bonds) as compared to stocks?**

   a. The lower return potential of bonds leads me to prefer stocks despite their higher volatility.

   b. Because bonds have the least volatility but also lower returns, I have a hard time choosing between the two.

   c. The high volatility of the stock market concerns me, so I prefer to invest in bonds.

5. **The three investments below represent three ways in which your money can be invested. Each shows returns from one year to the next. Which investment would you have chosen?**

	Year 1	Year 2
Investment A:	−20%	+30%
Investment B:	−15%	+25%
Investment C:	−5%	+15%

6. **You have $100,000 to invest. The following choices show a range of possible results of three types of investments at the end of one year. Which one would you choose?**

    a. Total value of $80,000–$140,000

    b. Total value of $90,000–$120,000

    c. Total value of $98,000–$108,000

7. **If the value of your portfolio decreased by 20% in one year, how would you react?**

    a. I would not be concerned about the short-term fluctuation in my investment.

    b. I would be somewhat concerned and would reconsider the aggressiveness of my portfolio.

    c. I would be very concerned, and I would find another way to invest my money.

8. **What is your overall knowledge of investments?**

    a. High. I have extensive experience in investing and have a broad understanding of capital markets in general.

    b. Medium. I have some experience investing in mutual funds or individual stocks and bonds.

    c. Low. I have very little investment experience outside of bank savings accounts, money market funds, and certificates of deposit (CDs).

Step 1: Scoring:

For questions: 1–2:

    a= 5 points

    b= 4 points

    c= 3 points

    d= 2 points

    e= 1 point

For all other questions

    a= 5 points

    b= 3 points

    c= 1 point

Step 2: Allocation Strategy Mapping

Tally up the point total for each of the three question sections and then combine the three subtotals for a grand total.

A. Time Horizon

    Question 1   _____

    Question 2   _____

        TOTAL POINTS   _____

B.Long-Term Goals and Expectations

    Question 3   _____

    Question 4   _____

    Question 5   _____

C. Short-Term Results

    Question 6   _____

    Question 7   _____

    Question 8   _____

    GRAND TOTAL (SECTIONS A, B, AND C)

        TOTAL POINTS   _____

Your type of portfolio should emphasize

8–12 Points Current Income

This is typical for the investor who is risk averse and wants current income and stability. The indication is that a low tolerance for risk is present yet you hope to protect principal asset value. Because you have liquidity requirements, this category is generally associated with a short-term time horizon.

13–18 Points Balanced

This is typical for the investor who primarily seeks income but wants a growth component as a hedge against inflation. The indication is that a moderate to low tolerance for risk is present. Because you have liquidity requirements, this category is generally associated with a short-term time horizon.

19–29 Points Growth and Income

This is typical for the investor who has a potential need for current income and wants reasonable but relatively stable investment growth. The indication is that some tolerance for risk and the desire for asset growth are present. Because you may have some liquidity requirements, this category is generally associated with a midterm time horizon.

30–35 Points Growth

This is typical for the investor who can accept a fair amount of risk but who may not be willing to accept large swings in volatility. The indication is that a reasonable tolerance for risk but possibly some liquidity requirements are present. This category is generally associated with a longer-term time horizon.

36–40 Points Maximum Growth

This is typical for the investor who is not in need of current income and is looking for high growth potential. The indication is that a high tolerance for risk and limited liquidity requirements are present. This category is generally associated with a longer-term time horizon.

5 How to Manage Your Assets over Time

Your goals and level of risk tolerance are the most significant aspects of investing. They drive the investment decisions that you will make, including your asset allocation, or how you will diversify among the various asset classes. In line with the results you are seeking and in conjunction with your style of investing (aggressive or conservative), you will want to allocate assets appropriately to meet your specific goals.

Many investors, often following the advice of advisors or even TV commercials, focus their attention on specific stocks, bonds, or mutual funds. People will see a rate of return and be ready to invest without factoring in the big-picture plan. This type of investing, chasing returns, doesn't work.

Instead, you need to ask yourself some key questions. For example: *Do I need income? How much? When? Am I looking for long-term growth? How much money do I need on hand in the form of liquid assets?* The answers lie within the broad investment picture. This larger picture is where you'll need to put your focus before thinking about specific investments.

When decorating your home, you wouldn't just select a carpet without determining which rooms you want covered with carpeting or without measuring the square footage of those rooms. First, you would determine the various options and consider how you want each room to look. You might opt for carpeting in three rooms, tile in the kitchen and bathrooms, and hardwood floors in the den. Therefore, before you go to Home Depot and/or your local carpet store, you will have already decided on the various floor coverings you want.

Likewise, before you invest, you will look at the various investment vehicles on a broad basis and determine how much you want to invest in each area on the basis of your needs. Start with a design based on what you need to accomplish.

Don't start by reading the most popular financial magazine and looking to buy the mutual fund that came in at number one the previous year. Concentrate on your needs. Should you put more money into equities (stocks) or into bonds? Should you consider other investment vehicles? These answers will be based on the "big picture."

Breaking It All Down

Asset allocation will vary for each individual. The idea is to allocate assets so that your goals are met and you feel comfortable with your investment strategy. After all, it's your money, your retirement, your lifestyle. Making sure your needs are met and your level of risk tolerance is taken into consideration are the priorities when allocating your assets. Stick with the strategy that meets your needs. If, for example, you need a 7% return to make your lifestyle work, then why take on the added risk by trying for a 20% return? You do not need to take on such a risk unless your position allows for it. Besides, if you have a low risk tolerance, you will probably get apoplexy on a roller-coaster ride you don't need to take.

I take it step by step when working with a client. Modern technology aside, I like to use a very simple approach that you can also use. I take a sheet of paper and draw three circles representing bags of money. One bag represents growth, which will be our growth component of the portfolio. The second bag represents income, for the long-term income needs. The third bag represents cash for liquidity, or to cover your immediate needs.

The three bags are independent of one another but work together to create an overall allocation and distribution strategy. The dollar amount in each bag is determined by available investable assets, risk tolerance, and annual income needs.

The cash bag will provide monthly income. There is limited market risk for these assets. Returns are generally more predictable in short-term investments despite market fluctuations. These dollars will earn short-term interest rates, and I don't really care what that rate is as long as the principal is safe. This provides a security blanket. Regardless of what happens in a 12- to 18-month period, our retirees know they have steady income for that time period.

The fixed-income bag will consist of assets that generate income such as bonds, utilities, or real estate investment trusts. A well-balanced allocation strives to replenish the immediate cash distributions with a consistent income stream. As we know, there is more volatility in the stock market in the short term, so this approach allows the stocks in the growth bag to remain in place to go through the ups and downs of market cycles. The goal is never to need to take money out of the equity market to generate income. The risk in doing so would be that someone would need money when the market is down. Ideally, money comes out of the equity market only when there's been appreciation that has been captured and moved to the bond portion to generate income or in some cases directly to the cash account. In this way, the bags work together in a specific manner.

AN EXAMPLE

Let's take a client who has $1 million in assets and $35,000 in income from Social Security and a pension. We have determined that he has a lifestyle that will need an additional income of $48,000 to cover all of his expenses.

First, we'll take $96,000 and put it into a cash account. Typically, this will be a money market account, where the return may be low but the dollars are safe and easily accessible. The Social Security and pension checks come to an additional $35,000 a year, $70,000 over two years. Combined, that $166,000 provides for two years of income. Regardless of what happens, our client knows he has two years of secure income. Wouldn't this added security make you feel good?

Because we are starting with two years of income in the bank, we will look at how to generate an income of $24,000 from the fixed-income portion. Bonds are a solid means of income and are typically "safer" investments, so we look at the fixed-income bag where we typically find bonds. If we calculate that bonds have historically generated a 6% rate of return, then we need to determine how much money at a 6% rate would replace $24,000. Using our handy calculator, we would get $400,000. Therefore, we would put $400,000 into bonds or income-generating investment vehicles. The remaining money ($1,000,000 - $400,000 - $96,000 = $504,000) would go into equities for growth. From day one, we know we have three years of income, with the additional $24,000 of income being generated from fixed income.

Remember that taking appreciation from stocks is also a strategy for providing income but not one that should be counted on from month to month, only over time. If the stock market has not provided any appreciation, such as from 2000 through 2002, then the principal of the bond portfolio may need to be invaded. By monitoring the portfolio on a regular basis, we will not arrive at the fourth year without having considered other options along the way. Also, we will need to adjust for inflation as time goes on and for any changes in tax laws. Again, with constant monitoring, there should not be any surprises.

Therefore, the 6% rate of return on the bonds will be used to replenish the cash while the equity portion continues to grow. Because many retirement funds are in IRAs or 401(k) accounts, there is no concern about capital gains taxes on the money accumulating from the equity portion of the portfolio.

Turning our attention back to asset allocation and the percentages allocated, in this example, we ended up with a 50-40 split of equities (growth) and bonds (income) with a small portion (10%) in cash for the purpose of liquidity.

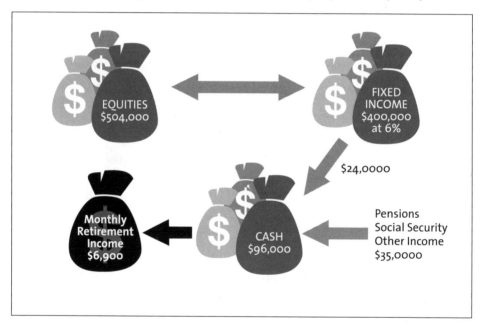

Monitoring Your Portfolio

The above example offers a simplistic way of looking at asset allocation, but it also provides an overall game plan that you can keep coming back to. It will, in time, be adjusted to stay in line with changes in your lifestyle and future plans as well as changes in market conditions. I recommend a six-month review, unless an emergency arises and there is a dramatic change in your immediate needs.

As you review every six months, you should ask yourself:

- Do I need more money?

- Can I manage on less money?

- Are my investments performing as anticipated?

- What market changes have an affect on my portfolio?

- What major expenses do I anticipate within the next two years?

Unless someone's lifestyle changes, or in the event that the investment vehicles we're using to generate income are not paying enough to get the percentage we're looking for, we will not make changes. When the bond market has higher rates of return compared to historical returns, we are able to reach income goals by investing less money in this category. Conversely, when equities do well and bonds are not doing as well, we are able to take some of the growth in equities and put it in bonds. This may seem counterproductive, but during the years 2000-2002, this proved to be a smart strategy.

While you need not make major or frequent changes, you'll change your asset allocation over time.

Investment Vehicles

Typically, I look at a combination of several investment vehicles, including:

- Stocks

- Mutual funds

- Bonds (including bond mutual funds)

- REITs (real estate investment trusts)

- Annuities

- Money market funds

We tend to use individual stocks only when a client has a substantial portfolio to handle the added risk. The idea is to take advantage of the greater diversification in an equity mutual fund and the expertise of a fund manager. Stockbrokers typically do not manage individual stocks with the same intensity as a fund manager. Equity mutual funds allow for much greater diversification and reduce the degree of risk.

Mutual Funds

The first equity mutual fund was established as far back as 1924 and consisted of 45 stocks. It wasn't, however, until the 1990s that mutual funds became the rage and fund managers became as popular, in some circles, as baseball stars. While the economic downturn of the past several years has taken the shine off the rosy picture of mutual fund madness, they should still remain a key component in your retirement portfolio.

Mutual funds, in short, are the sum of their many parts, which are the individual stocks within the fund. The fund manager does the buying, monitoring, and selling of the various equities and makes your job much easier because you need only select the type of fund that best meets your needs.

Benefits of mutual funds include:

- Instant diversification (by owning many stocks)

- Professional fund management

- Ease of purchasing

- Lower risk than individual stocks

A mutual fund also allows you to buy into many stocks with one payment, thus stretching your dollar further than you could by purchasing individual stocks. For example, a $10,000 investment in one mutual fund can buy you 200 stocks, where purchasing each stock individually would cost significantly more money and be far more difficult to monitor.

Within the mutual fund arena, there are many variations on the overall theme. There are literally thousands of funds to choose from, and a good advisor is worth his or her weight in gold if he or she can narrow the field down to the ones that are best suited for your needs.

Mutual funds, like stocks, are an investment that fluctuates with market conditions, and they do involve risk. Investment returns and principal value will fluctuate just as stocks do.

Making Bonds Work for You

For our purposes, we use bonds to help generate income. The types of bonds will depend in part on your income needs, as well as your risk tolerance and the current rates. Like equity mutual funds, bond funds can provide diversification. However, because bonds are typically less volatile and are easier to predict than stocks, bonds can be bought individually for your portfolio, with the guidance of a financial advisor.

As people approach retirement, the security of bonds often becomes more attractive. Diversification (between various types of bonds) is still recommended, as is always the case when investing.

You will also need to consider the different ways in which bonds pay interest. Fixed-interest bonds pay the same steady amount of interest and do not fluctuate. Bonds with variable interest rates, however, will fluctuate. Variable interest rates may be affected by economic conditions, exchange rates, and the stock market. Historically, the bond market will do well when the stock market does worse, and vice versa.

You've probably also heard of zero coupon bonds—not typically purchased within retirement accounts—which pay no interest but are sold at a deep discount and redeemed at full value. They build up through compounding of the interest. This doesn't serve the purpose of generating income as outlined above.

The interest from bonds provides your base retirement income coupled with Social Security and any other steady avenues of income, which might also include a monthly payout from a pension plan. One thing you need to be aware of with bonds is that their underlying value will fluctuate. But because we are buying bonds for the income they generate and not for their potential appreciation, the day-to-day fluctuations in value do not concern us greatly.

While many retirees move into new jobs or start new business ventures, it is typically best to focus primarily on bonds as the main source of steady income for your retirement portfolio. If you start a business that does well and provides income, you'll then have the very pleasant dilemma of figuring out what to do with the extra income. In the meantime, you should work within the three bags as outlined above.

A Bit about Buying/Selling Bonds

Bond mutual funds operate in a similar manner to stock funds, holding many bonds and buying and selling within the overall fund. Many factors influence the bond market. If, for example, you own a bond paying 8% and interest rates drop to 6%, your bond would then be in greater demand, so you may be able to sell your bond at a premium. Conversely, if you are holding the same 8% bond and the interest rates rise to 10%, your bond will be far less attractive to buyers. Potential buyers would be interested in your bond only if you were selling it at a discount. Therefore, lower interest rates usually mean higher bond prices, and higher interest rates usually mean lower bond prices. Your financial advisor should be keeping tabs on interest rates and which way they are likely to go.

Cash

I have noticed that the most common manner of maintaining cash today by my clients is in a money market account. Money markets have all but replaced the traditional bank account for many people because the returns are generally better than those on a typical savings account.

All the rage back in the late 1970s when they were new, today, money markets are investment vehicles in which you can feel confident about leaving available cash. These accounts are priced based at a rate of $1 per share, meaning the amount of dollars you have is the amount of shares you have. Investments in money market accounts are in safe havens, including short-term, high-quality obligations such as treasury bills and CDs. In fact, by law, money markets are prohibited from owning any long-term investments in their portfolios.

Typically, a money market account will also have check-writing privileges, so you can use it as your checking account as well.

Whether it's a money market or traditional bank account, the cash portion of your portfolio is not about rate of return but liquidity. It's about having money on hand to pay your bills.

Annuities

Annuities are essentially contracts sold by insurance companies that provide payments to the holder. All annuities are tax deferred, meaning that the holder will pay income tax on the gain only when he or she starts taking distributions or if he or she withdraws money from the account. There are three types of annuities: fixed, variable, and immediate. Fixed annuities pay a fixed interest rate for a set period of time. Variable annuities, which have been very popular over the past several years, allow the investor to choose between fixed rates, stock funds, and bond funds. There are almost as many options to these annuities as there are annuities from which to choose.

An immediate annuity provides a fixed income to the owner for life or for a certain number of years. In this scenario, the owner gives cash to the insurance company, and the company guarantees the income. Although this sounds good, the owner gives up control of the cash to the insurance company. Also, in a low-interest-rate environment, the return on these types of annuities can be very low.

There is much controversy about whether one should put retirement dollars into an annuity. The negative argument is based on the fact that retirement assets are already tax deferred, so why use annuities, particularly when they cost more than other types of investments?

Annuities are appropriate, I believe, in certain and specific cases regardless of whether the dollars used to purchase the annuity are in a retirement account or an individual account, meaning any income or capital gain is taxed in the current year. For example, take a case where a wife might be very fearful of the stock market but needs growth in her portfolio. She is afraid that her husband will die and she won't have enough money available to last her lifetime. An annuity provides protection in the form of a death benefit that will pay whatever the contributor put into the annuity or the value of the account, whichever is greater. Therefore, if the husband dies, the widow is guaranteed to get whatever was put into the annuity. If, for example, he put $100,000 in an annuity contract and the value had dropped to $80,000 when he died, his spouse would still get the $100,000 that was initially invested. If, however, the value of the annuity had gone up $20,000 in value, then she would receive $120,000.

Variable annuities work well during a down market; they provide a guarantee, which is good for someone looking for growth but uncomfortable with unstable market conditions. This is a perfect example where risk tolerance and client needs can be met with one investment vehicle. A client with a very low risk tolerance but who needs to take on higher risk to meet his or her long-term needs will be well suited to this investment.

Be careful of "experts" making statements about various investment vehicles, particularly annuities. Remember that they have no vested interest your situation nor do they understand the fears you may be confronting.

There are additional charges and fees inherent in annuities. Nonetheless, if you are conservative by nature, annuities can be particularly attractive. Contrary to much of the negative publicity surrounding variable annuities, they can provide a benefit to the nervous investor.

Like IRAs, withdrawals from an annuity prior to age 59½ will cause a 10% penalty to be incurred. In addition, withdrawals of the growth of an annuity are taxed at ordinary income tax rates. However, if you are using qualified retirement funds in the annuity, those dollars are already taxed at ordinary income tax rates, so this should not be considered a disadvantage.

Annuities come with a multitude of options, all of which can add to the cost of the investment. You need to be sure that you understand the features, the cost, and the benefit of each.

Real Estate

Typically, when we talk about real estate investing, we're not talking about buying that lovely ranch-style home just outside of town and renting it out. Too many headaches. Instead, we are talking about REITs (pronounced REETs), which are real estate investment trusts.

A somewhat lesser-known means of investing, REITs provide a way to invest in real estate in a manner similar to investing in a stock or bond mutual fund. Mutual fund REITs allow you to invest in real estate companies rather than buying (and being responsible for) actual land or property. In addition, the investment is liquid because you can sell off shares just as you would do with a stock or mutual fund. Created by an act of Congress in 1960, REITs are publicly traded companies that purchase mortgages, rental properties, and/or other real estate or invest in real estate–related businesses. They are professionally managed, and many hold several pieces of real estate, sometimes as many as 100 or more properties.

REITs are also pass-through investment vehicles, meaning they pass income through to shareholders and retain no earnings. This means that you are responsible for paying the taxes unless you are investing under the umbrella of a tax-exempt retirement account such as your IRA or 401(k), which you should be utilizing to build your retirement portfolio.

We use the income generated from REITs much in the same manner as that generated from bonds or bond funds. Depending on the rates, we will look at both asset classes to generate the steady income that you need. As is the case with bonds, we will use the interest generated from a REIT to regularly replenish the cash account. Thus, a REIT can provide another excellent source of income.

Some individual REITs are publicly traded on the NYSE, and although they generally pay an attractive dividend, they do act like a stock. These types of individual REITs or a mutual fund of REITs would be included in the equity portion of your allocation bag. Before REITs go public, they are considered nonpublicly traded because there is no secondary market where they can be sold. This is the initial stage of a publicly traded REIT. During this phase, the value of the REIT does not rise and fall with market conditions because it cannot be traded. These types of REITs we would include in the fixed-income bag until such time as they go public. These may be appropriate to purchase when the publicly traded REITs are overpriced. Again, your advisor should be able to direct you as to the best time to buy any of these vehicles.

Other Investments

We typically steer clear of other investments such as options, futures, or higher-risk ventures in retirement plans. Often, such investments require specific expertise in the area and greater monitoring. Therefore, the need for income and growth from a retirement plan is generally served best by the above-mentioned retirement vehicles.

No Set Formula and No "Sure Things"

Mutual fund companies today offer what are called lifestyle funds, which are mutual funds that invest on the basis of the age of the investors. They become progressively more conservative as investors get older. The problem with such funds is that no two people have the exact same lifestyle. In addition, people of all ages have different goals, needs, and levels of risk tolerance. The theory of changing asset allocation strictly on the basis of someone's age does not work for most investors.

One client of mine, for example, is in her 70s, and she's worth more than $2 million. With Social Security and a pension, she takes only $15,000 a year from her assets, so she's not about to run out of money. She's investing for the benefit of leaving money to her children and grandchildren. Why should she become a conservative investor because of her age? She's hoping to build up a sizable amount of funds to leave for her heirs.

People have very different lifestyles that need to be factored into their asset allocation strategy at any age. Therefore, age becomes just one of a number of factors when determining someone's asset allocation. Additionally, people have very different levels of risk tolerance, which is always a key factor when setting up an investment plan.

There is no set one-size-fits-all investment strategy. The best strategy for anyone planning to invest, whether it is for retirement or any other goal, is to do some homework and read about an investment opportunity before taking the plunge. A good financial advisor should help a client put an investment game plan in place before investing any money.

Sticking to your own set plan can take some willpower when it becomes tempting to go after a "sure thing." As we mentioned back at the start of the chapter, chasing returns doesn't work. Just because your next-door neighbor had a 30% return on a mutual fund doesn't mean you will. In fact, it's highly unlikely. It also doesn't mean you can afford to (or even want to) take such a risk. Stick to your own game plan. There are no formulas and no "sure things" when it comes to investing.

Common Mistakes

There are a variety of mistakes that investors make in managing their assets, and most of them are related to behavior.

1. **Greed:** In 1998 and 1999, when getting a 30% return on a mutual fund was ho-hum, everyone was racing to the technology stock with the highest return, 80% to 100%. No one wanted to miss out, and the usually conservative, reasonable investor was in the middle of it all. "I don't want those stinkin' bonds; they are yielding only 7%" was the common mantra. Give me technology and NOW!

2. **Fear:** The opposite of greed has equally damaging psychological problems. "Get me out now! I can't take any more losses. Let's sit it out until the market has bottomed out, and then I'll go back in." As if anyone would know when the bottom had arrived. The emotions are real, but acting on them generally is inappropriate.

3. **Overdiversification:** If one is good, then 20 is better. Many portfolios are made of the number-one-performing fund of the previous year. Eventually, you have a variety of funds or stocks that all look the same.

4. **Underdiversification:** This goes hand in hand with greed: betting the farm on one or two stocks, looking for the grand slam. It is a roll of the dice at best, and the risks are high. Many, many people have gotten caught in this emotion with their company stock—Enron and Worldcom to name a few. I still see many people with the majority of their 401(k) in their company stock but who consider themselves moderate to conservative investors. They think those bad things will not happen to them.

5. **Borrowing:** Using someone else's money to leverage your position can be a smart investment move. We do it all the time when buying a home. But taking on this additional risk in the equity market is a recipe for disaster, especially as you near retirement.

   As Warren Buffett's teacher Benjamin Grahman said in his book *The Intelligent Investor*, "The investor's chief problem—and even his worst enemy—is likely to be himself."

Prior to Retirement

Prior to retirement, you should have already found a financial advisor with whom you feel comfortable. In fact, I recommend starting several years in advance for two reasons. First, you want to be sure the advisor is right for you. Over the course of several meetings, you can get a feeling of whether the advisor is planning a retirement strategy that meets your specific needs. Second, you want to be sure you have a workable plan in place, and this can take some time to prepare and develop.

Logistics

Rolling Funds from Your Company to Your IRA

Depending on the company you have been working for, how you initiate the process of transferring your 401(k) profit sharing or lump sum pension will vary.

Most companies will provide the necessary forms that will give you the various options that are available and the consequences of each. Although this paperwork may seem overwhelming, the forms you will be completing are relatively simple.

The key questions are:

- Do you want to take the money out of the 401(k) plan or leave it there?

- If you take it out, how do you go about doing so?

- How do you avoid taxes and penalties?

If your plan is to roll the funds into an IRA, which is generally recommended, then the administrator of the plan will want to know to whom the check will be made payable. The check should be made payable to your new custodian chosen by you and your advisor. The key is to roll over the funds without having the check payable to you. If the check is made out to you, you will be subjected to 20% withholding for income taxes. When you file your tax return, you will pay ordinary income tax on the amount distributed. In addition, if you are under the age of 501/2, you will incur an additional 10% penalty.

If you are over the age of 55 and your employment has been terminated, you can leave the funds in the 401(k) at your company and take distributions without the 10% penalty. You will still need to pay ordinary income tax. If you think you'll need some of the funds prior to reaching 59½, this may be a good option.

You can also pull money out of an IRA without penalties before the age of 59½ by taking equal and substantial payments over a five-year period or until you are 59½, whichever is greater. If, for example, you start taking money out at age 56, you would have to take the same amount of money out each year until you were 61. The amount required to take under these IRS rules is determined on the basis of your life expectancy. While money can be taken out if necessary, I do not recommend that you start withdrawing from a retirement plan too early because you will potentially need the money for many years to come. Remember, we are living longer than in previous generations.

As for pension plans, companies typically offer either a lump sum or a monthly benefit. There are some drawbacks to monthly benefits. First, while the benefit can go to your spouse should you die, there is no provision for where the money will go when both you and your spouse die. Also, if the corporation does not provide for a cost of living increase, which most don't, then your monthly benefit will be worth less over time. Another concern, especially today with many companies struggling to stay afloat, is what if the company goes bankrupt? While pension plans are guaranteed through the Pension Benefit Guarantee Corporation, the insurance coverage will not match the plan dollar for dollar, so again, you'll end up receiving less money. Therefore, I almost always advise that you take a lump sum pension payment. You'll need to roll it over into an IRA and be careful about how you manage it, but you'll have the full amount at your disposal, and also have the benefit of passing these funds to your beneficiaries after the death of you and your spouse.

Making Your Legacy Come Alive: An Introduction to Estate Planning

6

A retirement plan would not be complete without addressing estate planning. My approach is to be sure that my clients have considered everything that needs to be done so that they can travel and enjoy their retirement while knowing that there are no loose ends that have not been addressed.

Leaving a legacy behind, writing a will, and establishing a trust are all touchy subjects that many of us tend to avoid. After all, when they serve to benefit our heirs, it means that we are no longer in the picture.

One of the most basic aspects of estate planning is that of making a will. From a practical perspective, the process is not difficult. It is, however, an emotional hurdle for many people. The process requires thinking through where you want everything to go and whom you want handling your estate after you are gone. Before you can determine who gets what, you have to know what makes up your estate. For example, many people do not realize that the value of their life insurance policy is a part of their estate and can increase the total of the estate substantially if they are the owners of the policy.

Besides setting up a will, it is also imperative that people go back and update their wills periodically. I have clients come to see me who wrote a will 20 years ago but have not reviewed it since. Many aspects of life change over time, and this will impact the will. For example, someone who divorces and remarries will want to change the name of his or her beneficiary to his or her children, parents, or new spouse. A new son-in-law, daughter-in-law, or grandchild may be added to the list of beneficiaries, while other beneficiaries may pass away and need to be taken out of the will. Therefore, I recommend to my clients that they review their will every three to four years or when major life changes occur to make sure it is up to date. They should also review who the beneficiaries are on 401(k)s and IRAs on a regular basis.

In the course of not wanting to deal with the subjects of estate planning and writing a will, people are also very often protective of their children, not wanting to worry them by bringing up such an emotional subject. The problem, however, that often arises is that those heirs are often left with the very difficult, often tenuous task of trying to track down and find important information such as bank account numbers, keys for safe-deposit boxes, insurance information, and so on. The combination of an emotionally stressful time coupled with the practical and logistical problems of trying to get everything organized can be very trying. Clients often say that after someone has passed away, it took months to locate personal information and sort out the details.

One client of mine living in Illinois was named executor of his aunt's estate. She, however, had resided in Florida. It took him some six months of traveling back and forth while trying to locate all of her assets and documentation to complete an inventory of her estate. No one had a sense of where she kept her personal information, and whenever he thought he had everything in order, he'd get a call or a letter from someone or a bill. When he was finally done straightening out all the elements of her estate, he understood why I had constantly been after him to put all of his own personal information in order using our legacy-planning document. He realized that trying to find all of the information that makes up someone's estate can be like trying to put together a jigsaw puzzle without all of the pieces. In addition, the emotional issues that arise when dealing with the loss of a close relative make the process even that much more trying and stressful.

For the sake of trying to organize such materials, I've included a "Legacy Profile" as a checklist or gathering point for organizing such information at the end of this chapter. You might give this to your own parents to fill out or fill it out and give a copy to your grown children for safekeeping. The most important aspect of leaving a legacy is that your intended beneficiaries receive the benefit from your estate.

Many of my clients have safe-deposit boxes. When I ask them who, besides them, knows about or has access to the safe-deposit box, inevitably, they say no one. Remember that planning should be done assuming the worst-case scenario. Make the assumption that if you are married, you may both die in an accident, and if you are single, assume that you will not have the chance to speak to someone before you die. Organization and planning are very significant.

Life Insurance

Life insurance is a key component of your estate plan. Many people don't think of adding this to their net worth when calculating their potential estate tax. It is, however, part of the estate plan.

Do you have life insurance? Do you need it?

I generally tell people that there are three basic reasons to have life insurance. One reason is for survivorship income. Survivorship income is typically needed if there are young children or minors who need to be supported and a lifestyle that has been maintained by two incomes. This is not usually part of a retirement scenario but more commonly necessary for "younger" couples.

A second reason for life insurance is in the event a spouse's retirement income or pension disappears at death. If one spouse's retirement income or pension is terminated with the death of that spouse, the surviving spouse may need to replace that income to maintain his or her lifestyle. Life insurance can prove beneficial in such a circumstance.

The third reason why someone may choose to hold onto life insurance is if an individual has a substantial net worth and there is a potential for estate taxes. In this case, I'd recommend having life insurance to protect assets from taxation. In the case of a husband and wife, they're allowed under current law to pass everything to either spouse with no estate taxes due. The problem comes in at the second death. If an individual estate is more than $1.5 million (as of 2005), everything over the $1.5 million is exposed to the estate tax, which starts at around 45%. You can't avoid this tax unless you give your assets away, which can come in various forms.

You can, however, preserve your estate by buying life insurance to pay for the estate taxes. It is much less expensive to purchase life insurance to cover the impending estate tax than to pay the death taxes out of your estate. More on managing your estate will be discussed later.

Essentially, if you're in a position to retire today with enough income (for both of you) and assuming the income you're getting today will continue with the death of one of you, then you may not have a need for life insurance. If life insurance is not costing you anything, I would probably leave it in place. However, the cash value of a life insurance policy can help significantly to fund long-term health care, which could be of greater need at this time.

People are often hesitant to let go of life insurance. It's been preached that they need it, and it is there in case something should happen. They bought it to protect their family, so there's a sense that it is still an umbrella, protecting them just in case. From a practical standpoint, however, it may not be worth keeping, and those dollars can be redirected by reducing expenses or using the cash value for other needs.

Trusts

Unless you have more than $1.5 million or real estate in other states, you may not need a living trust if you own everything jointly as a married couple. Upon the death of the first spouse, everything will pass to the surviving spouse smoothly without the need for probate. At that time, a trust would be very beneficial. If, however, you own assets individually, you may be required to go through the probate process. The problem with probate is that it is a process that can take anywhere from 6 to 18 months. This can be costly and can leave your heirs in limbo during this time period. Therefore, you may want to set up a trust primarily to avoid the probate process and help make sure that everything goes smoothly and specifically where you intend it to go in a reasonable amount of time.

Often, people don't want to spend the $2,000 or $3,000 to set up such a trust. It will be worthwhile in that it makes things easier for heirs, who are already going through a difficult emotional time. A trust allows a person to spell out in greater detail how the money is to be managed and distributed. In addition to expediting the process by avoiding probate, a trust is a private matter. Probate involves going through the courts and therefore goes on public record. When dealing with very large estates, such information can become a point of contention and may be best kept out of the public eye.

There are many similar common misconceptions about trusts. First, it is widely believed that a trust is complicated to set up. In reality, it is usually no more complex than setting up a will. The writing of the document should be in the hands of a qualified attorney, who will walk you through the process. You will want to determine over what period of time you want your property to be distributed, the beneficiaries who will receive the property, and the trustees who will manage the trust assets. This can usually be addressed in a couple of meetings with a qualified advisor and attorney.

Another misconception is that by setting up a trust, you will lose control of your assets. This is simply not true. Having a revocable trust means you can and will retain total control over and will continue to have the same ease of use of your assets. The investments are simply held in the name of the trust, but you do not give up ownership. In addition, a revocable trust can be changed at any time.

In contrast, by using an irrevocable trust, you will give up ownership. These trusts are used to remove assets from your estate today. This can be useful in certain circumstances such as with a life insurance policy. We discussed earlier the use of life insurance to cover the estate tax cost. However, if you purchase the life insurance in your name, the death benefit proceeds will be included in your estate. This could result in 40% to 50% of those proceeds going to the IRS. By setting up an irrevocable life insurance trust, you have no ownership of the life insurance. When you pass away, that money is not included in your estate and, therefore, is not subject to estate tax. In such a situation, you do not need to have control over the trust anyway because the money from the life insurance policy will not become available until after you are gone. One item to note is that if you transfer an existing policy into an irrevocable life insurance trust, there is a three-year look-back rule. In other words, if you die within three years of transferring the policy, it will be included in your estate.

The third misconception about revocable living trusts is that they circumvent the need to pay estate taxes. Unfortunately, this one is also not the case.

Gifting

One way of keeping money away from the estate tax collectors is to give it away. That's right—give it away. Gifting is a means whereby you can give away up to $11,000 per year (as of 2005) without gift tax to as many people as you choose, typically family and loved ones. The person who receives the gift pays no income tax on the gift. Deciding whether to begin a gifting program should first require that you have a discussion with your financial advisor.

Before starting a gifting program with my clients, I take a look at their net worth and spending habits to help make sure they aren't going to run out of money. In many cases, I find that if clients are earning more in their investments than they are using for income needs, there could be a reason for looking at a gifting program.

A gifting program can also change from year to year. For example, one client of mine in her late 50s gifts in certain years and doesn't gift in others depending on how the market is doing and how much she's earning. I want to make sure that she'll have enough money if she lives to be 100. Obviously, the older you are, the easier it is to do the calculations because life expectancy becomes shorter.

It should also be noted that while you're entitled to give away $11,000 per year, per person, without paying gift tax, $1 million of your estate tax exemption ($1.5 million is exempt in 2005) can also be given away during your lifetime. In some cases, instead of giving away $11,000 per year, I will recommend gifting more and having it applied to the $1.5-million estate exclusion that each individual is entitled to. Any gifts over $1 million during the course of your lifetime will be subject to gift tax.

For example, if I have a client with $3 million in assets and he or she is 75 years old, there could be more than enough money to support his or her lifestyle for the balance of his or her life. In fact, if the assets are growing quickly, then it might be better, for estate tax purposes, to give away the $1 million today. That will freeze the $1 million so it can't increase in value in the client's estate. It will also pass on to the beneficiaries today rather than after the client dies.

It is important, however, to determine what you are gifting. While cash allows you to make the smoothest transition, stocks can be more complicated. For example, if you bought stocks at $5 per share and the stock went up to $10 per share, when gifting $11,000 worth of shares, the person to whom you have gifted the shares of stocks will pay income taxes on the amount over the $5 per share that you paid for the stock when he or she sells the stock. This person is, in effect, being taxed not on the value of the stock at the time of gifting but on the full increase in value of the shares since the stock was originally purchased. If the stock went up to $14 per share and the recipient of the gift sold the stock, he or she would pay capital gains taxes on the $9 per share profit because that is how much the per-share value of the stock increased since the original purchase.

If, however, you held the stock and left it to be inherited, the law states that the basis of the stock would be that at which it was when inherited. If the price was $14 per share at the death of the owner and it was sold immediately for $14 by the beneficiary, then there would be no income tax due. There would be taxes due only on the amount over the $14 inherited value.

It's worth keeping in mind that highly appreciated stock is great for gifting to charities because they do not pay taxes.

Yes, it can become more complicated, but gifting can work to lessen inheritance taxes and put money into the hands of the people you wish to have it while you are still around.

When you get into this phase of estate planning, you need to sit down with a qualified financial advisor who can help you carefully lay out the steps. There are many different ways in which you can plan out gifting programs and trusts. You can also do some wonderfully creative things and leave a legacy for many generations to come.

One gentleman I've worked with is a widower with two children. He has significant assets and a passion for music. Being a charitably inclined individual, he wanted to set aside money to be donated to music schools. So, we established a charitable trust whereby money could be donated to music schools for many years to come, even long after he passed away. This will create a legacy where his money will be used to enhance the talents of future generations of students in an area that he was always passionate about while still leaving significant assets for his children.

Estate Taxes

They say there are only two things you can be sure of, death and taxes, and estate tax combines them both. Ironically, estate taxes are actually **not** something you can be sure of. As of the year 2005, you can leave heirs $1.5 million tax free. And, as it turns out, the way the laws are now structured, this will increase to $3.5 million by 2009. In 2010, there will be no estate tax, and in 2011, the law reverts back to the laws of 2003, where you could pass $1 million estate tax free. Of course, the subject of estate taxes is often discussed in Congress, especially as the deficit grows. It is, therefore, safe to say that such laws could be repealed and many changes could occur over the next several decades.

The only solution to avoiding estate taxes is to give money away, as discussed above in "Gifting." Short of that option, you can minimize your estate taxes only if you are married by dividing your assets so you can both take advantage of the $1.5-million exclusion (as of 2005). Remember, assets that are owned joint with rights of survivorship (JTWROS) do not qualify for the exclusion. You must own them individually in your own name or as tenants in common.

The tools and means available to minimize estate taxes beyond the reregistering of assets can, in some cases, be complex. This book is not intended to address each method but to make you aware that should you have a problem, it is likely there is a solution.

One thing we can be sure of is that the estate tax laws as they stand today will surely change. This makes planning difficult and certainly requires that we review your estate plans regularly. Tax laws are subject to frequent change. The foregoing information is also based upon current understanding of today's tax laws and should not be construed as legal advice.

State Taxes on Inheritance

While the federal government does not impose inheritance taxes on the beneficiaries receiving money and properties from the deceased, several state governments do. Such taxes may be in addition to the state and federal estate tax. Each beneficiary is responsible for paying such taxes.

The financial deficit that so many states are now facing has brought up the question of raising estate taxes on a state-by-state basis. Several state governments are discussing this tax increase as a means of offsetting some of their financial woes. Therefore, suffice it say, because both federal and state taxes are changing all the time, it is worthwhile to monitor the situation or at least discuss the ongoing changes in estate and inheritance taxes with your financial advisor to best determine how you might reposition your estate plans. Select a financial advisor who is familiar with estate planning and who can explain your dangers and options. You want to be able to talk about how you can pass on a legacy as easily as you paint the portrait of your retirement years.

Planning Is the Key

What many parents fail to realize is that their planning will have an impact on their children. Therefore, communicating your plans can both relieve your children if you are financially independent and help them in their own estate planning. For example, if you are leaving several hundred thousand dollars to already successful heirs, you may just be increasing their estate problems down the road. Open discussions among family members can pave the path for estate planning that will not only minimize the taxes at your death but also pass on an estate tax-free legacy for grandchildren and beyond.

Having discussed estate planning and outlining your retirement goals and plans, we will proceed to look at putting all the elements together through a case study in the next chapter, which illuminates how I use the Total Vision Approach.

The Total Vision Approach

LEGACY PLANNING

Throughout a lifetime, each family member makes a valuable contribution. But when a family member dies, how do the survivors cope and get past this difficult time?

One way to help is by creating a document that can help make the transition somewhat easier. The emotional impact of losing a loved one can be devastating, and the added pressure of hunting down documents and important papers creates additional stress. **The Legacy Plan** presented here can assist you and your loved ones by making the transition as smooth as possible.

In an effort to make gathering all legal and personal documents easier, here I present an information source that can be used as a guide. Once completed, this material should be kept in a safe place made known only to specific family members or friends. You should provide your financial advisor with an additional copy. Your advisor should also remind you periodically that you can and should make necessary changes to the document over time as new situations develop and information about additional documents needs to be added.

This is a very caring way to help your family members through what will likely be one of their most trying periods.

Records	Location	Address
Birth Certificates		
Military Service Records		
Household Financial Records		

Records	Location	Address
Tax Records & Receipts		
W-2 Forms & other records of Earnings		
Car Registration & Title		
Wills		
V.A. Claim Number		
Social Security Numbers		
Employment Records		
Real Estate Deeds		
Bankbook Checkbook		
Certificates of Deposit		
Business Agreements or Contracts		
Software Passwords, Codes		
Safe-Deposit Boxes		
Other		
Other		

Family Records and Information
About the Family

My name _____

  Place and date of birth _____

Spouse's/partner's name _____

  Spouse's/partner's place and date of birth _____

Children (*full name, place and date of birth*)

_____

_____

_____

_____

Other family (*full name, place and date of birth*)

_____

_____

Family Records Location

Medical records _____

Birth certificates _____

Marriage certificate(s) _____

Military service records _____

Other important family records (nonfinancial, personal)

_____

_____

_____

Tax records and receipts _____

W-2 forms and other records of earnings _____

_____

Vehicle registrations and titles _____

Wills and trusts_____

Safe-deposit boxes

It is held in my name only.

It is held jointly with _____

Box number _____

Name and location of bank _____

_____

Location of keys _____

Life Insurance

I have the following life and life/long-term-care insurance policies:

_____

_____

_____

*If any policies listed are survivorship (last-to-die) plans, it is also important to notify insurer:

Other Family members	Insurance Company	Policy Number	Face Value

Government Life Insurance

I served in the (branch of service) _____
from _____ to _____ and received the following type of
discharge: _____

My serial number was _____

The status of my government life insurance is as follows
(*expired or still in force: face amount*): _____

_____

The policy is located at: _____

Trust(s) that I have set up:

_____

_____

_____

The bank, trust company, or other fiduciary _____

Trust officer _____

Telephone number _____

The trust is funded _____ unfunded _____.

Trust(s) my spouse has set up:

_____

_____

_____

The bank, trust company, or other fiduciary _____

Trust officer _____

Telephone number _____

The trust is funded _____ unfunded _____.

Real Estate Owned

Our home is at _____

It is owned jointly by _____

   singly by_____

Mortgagor_____

_____

   Telephone number _____

Location of mortgage or deed _____

_____

We have a second home at _____

_____

It is owned jointly by _____

   singly by_____

Mortgagor_____

_____

   Telephone number _____

Location of mortgage or deed _____

_____

Other real estate owned (excluding business, farm, or other enterprise)

_____

_____

_____

_____

_____

Bank Accounts (include savings and loan associations, credit union)

Checking, Savings or Certificates of Deposit	Account Number	Joint or Individual	Name & Location

Location of passbooks, checkbooks, canceled checks, and statements

_____

_____

_____

Stocks, Bonds, and Securities Portfolio

_____

_____

_____

Additional Financial Information

_____

_____

_____

Major debts (other than first mortgages and revolving charge accounts)

_____

_____

_____

Money owed to us:

_____

_____

_____

Location of notes payable and receivable

_____

_____

_____

Other information:

_____

_____

_____

People to Notify
Relatives and Friends

Upon my death, the following people should be notified immediately (names, addresses, and telephone numbers of closest relatives including those who, in turn, will notify others):

_____

_____

_____

_____

_____

_____

Confidential Advisors

Upon my death, the following people should be notified (names, addresses, and telephone numbers of physician, attorney, accountant, executor, employer, or business partner, etc.):

_____

_____

_____

_____

_____

_____

Upon my spouse's death, the following people should be notified:

_____

_____

_____

_____

Funeral and Burial Preferences

My personal funeral and burial preferences are:

_____

_____

_____

My wishes with regard to donating organs (including information on any arrangements that have been made):

_____

_____

_____

My spouse's personal funeral and burial preferences are

_____

_____

_____

My spouse's wishes in regard to donating organs (including information on any arrangements that have been made)

_____

_____

_____

Business, Farm, or Other Enterprise Information

Name of business _____

Kind of business

_____

_____

Location

_____

_____

Percentage of ownership (%) _____

Form of business (sole proprietorship, partnership, corporation)

_____

_____

Other owners (if any)

_____

_____

Is the business subject to a buy/sell agreement?

_____

_____

Information on other business interests or farms owned

_____

_____

Arrangements that have been made (or should be made after my death) in continuing or disposing of each business interest

_____

_____

Location of business books, records, and pertinent papers

_____

_____

Additional information

_____

_____

_____

Person or persons who could offer sound advice in carrying on the business or operating the farm or in disposing of the business or farm (names, addresses, and telephone numbers)

_____

_____

Credit Cards

Credit Card	Account Number	Phone Number

The above legacy plan is an organizational way of pulling everything together. It is a key step in estate planning and consolidating information. Estate planning is all about putting things together for your beneficiaries. You want to protect the legacy you've created and make sure things pass along smoothly, efficiently, and easily, minimizing estate taxes wherever possible.

A married couple typically has a lesser concern because the estate will typically pass smoothly from one spouse to the other. However, at the second death, or in the event both spouses die at the same time, arrangements need to be more carefully put into place.

Your hope is to have a legacy that passes assets on easily to children and grandchildren. You don't want to leave a situation where your wishes are not carried out. There are many stories about very wealthy people passing away and because their estates were not in order, many legal hassles ensued, and a substantial amount of money was lost to estate taxes.

Putting It All Together: A Case Study

7

Thus far, you've read about how to envision your retirement goals and set up a game plan. We've discussed the importance of knowing exactly what your spending needs are now and what you anticipate them to be in the future. We've also looked at various investment options and discussed the importance of assessing your own level of risk tolerance. In addition, we've taken into account the need for estate planning.

Now, in this chapter, we will put all of the pieces together as I do when a client begins discussing his or her retirement future. The result is the Total Vision Plan for retirement, mentioned in the beginning of the book.

Meet Bill and Mary

In this chapter, I will take you through the story of Mary and Bill Clark and their retirement scenario. They are typical of many of the clients that I meet. They are looking to retire, have been saving for years, and now want to know how to make all of their hard work pay off with a retirement plan that will satisfy their goals and meet their needs.

Bill is 62 years old, and Mary is 57. He works for Astor Labs and has been there for more than 30 years. His current salary is $75,000. Mary works part time at a local office doing primarily administrative work and earns $18,000 a year. She was a stay-at-home mom with their three daughters for many years and finally started working when the older and middle daughters were in college to help them pay their tuition.

Their combined household income is $93,000, or just over $60,000 after taxes. On the basis of our initial discussions, they indicated that their annual expenses totaled just over $40,000.

Investable assets for Bill and Mary include a 401(k) plan from Astor Labs* now totaling $650,000, of which $475,000 is in Astor Labs stock. The balance has been in aggressive-growth mutual funds. Upon retiring, Bill is going to roll his 401(k) plan over into an IRA.

Their savings, basically in short-term CDs, is $75,000. In addition, Mary has an IRA worth $26,000. They have been diligent at saving, slightly reducing the monthly amount invested for a short time during their daughters' college years.

Bill has a pension plan that will pay $1,700 per month for Bill's lifetime or $1,500 per month for both he and Mary's lifetime. The plan does not provide for inflation, and the amount will therefore not increase. On the basis of their IRS statements, Social Security for Bill will be $1,200 per month starting now and $600 per month for Mary when she is eligible at age 62.

Their home is valued at $225,000, and there is a $35,000 mortgage. Bill has a group term life insurance of $150,000 through work. Mary has no life insurance. They also have a very old whole life policy on Bill with a death benefit of $75,000 and cash value of $43,000.

Astor Labs will continue to provide Bill and Mary with health insurance after his retirement, and he will pay approximately $125 per month to continue the coverage.

There is no long-term health care plan in place, and while they both have wills, neither has been updated since 1983.

The Clarks' total net worth is $776,000, not including their house, which falls into the noninvestable assets category and totals $190,000 (including the mortgage).

*Astor Labs is a pseudonym for actual stocks owned by the couple on which this story is based.

More than Just Numbers

Bill and Mary have worked for many years, and both are ready to retire. They are, however, both scared and overwhelmed at the prospect of retirement. Their biggest fear is that they are going to run out of money. They want to be reassured that they are making the right decision and will have enough money throughout the retirement years that lie ahead. It is important to them that they maintain their standard of living without ever becoming dependant on their children for support.

They have seen their three daughters grow and move on. Their oldest daughter, Trisha, is single and enjoys a lucrative career heading a small marketing firm. Angela, their middle daughter, is married and is a stay-at-home mom with three children. Her husband works for a bank, and they just get by, meeting their expenses and having very little money to save. Her husband's future at the bank looks very promising, and they are very comfortable with their future. Both daughters are in regular contact with their parents, and neither is dependant on her parents for money. The third and youngest daughter, Janine, was always a bit more rebellious. Some five years younger than Angela, she was not particularly close to her sisters and went off on her own to study drama. Bill and Mary have not heard from her in two years, and their attempts to contact her usually fall flat because she moves around the West Coast. She has touched base with Trisha on occasion, so they know nothing horrible has happened to her. After college, Janine had problems with the use of drugs, and Bill and Mary are worried that she might be involved with drugs again.

Bill and Mary would like to consider gifting to their daughters but need to make sure it's the right approach. At the very least, they want to leave the girls a legacy.

Neither Bill nor Mary has given significant thought to retiring other than worrying about whether they could afford to do so. What would their lifestyle be? They have not considered, in great detail, what they would do to occupy their time. Because they live several thousand miles away from their daughters, spending time with family and seeing their grandchildren would not be part of their regular routine, but their family time would continue to include highly anticipated holiday and summer visits.

Neither Bill nor Mary is the type to sit back and put his or her feet up. They are both active, and retiring to a sedentary lifestyle would not suit either of them. I recommended that they both sit down and picture their retirement, as we discussed in Chapter 2. I wanted to get an idea of what they enjoy doing and what would occupy their time. Neither expressed an interest in pursuing a new career, but both returned with some definite ideas.

Bill discussed his passion for woodworking, a skill that he learned from his father, who had been a professional woodworker. It seems that Bill had enjoyed the craft very much in his 20s and even 30s but had lost the time for it many years ago with the responsibilities of work and family life. He was now excited at the prospect of setting up a woodworking shop in the garage and making items for friends, family, and just for himself. The idea that this passion could turn into a small business was also in the back of his mind.

Mary, meanwhile, wanted to do volunteer work at a local drug rehabilitation center. Having helped Janine through her first bout with drugs several years ago, she saw first hand the struggle that many people face, and this stirred her passion for helping others get through such a crisis.

This information was forthcoming from Bill and Mary in our first interview together. While none of this information has dollar signs attached to it, it was an integral part of the planning process.

Concerns for Bill and Mary

Through our discussions, several concerns emerged in my mind for Bill and Mary. First, we needed to evaluate the discrepancy between how much money they were taking home and what they said were their current spending needs. My concern was that they were not taking everything into account. It is very typical when someone begins listing annual expenses to leave things out. There are many smaller expenses that we tend not to consider. Fixed expenses such as mortgage payments, car payments, and utility bills are easily identifiable. Discretionary expenses such as clothing, gifts, and entertainment are generally understated or many times totally forgotten.

The next concern was that the majority of their assets were in one stock and there was virtually no diversification. Like many clients who have enjoyed great success over the years with a stock from their company, Bill expressed his reluctance to let go. It is important not to become emotionally attached to any investment. The Astor stock had been very good to them and continued to do fairly well in recent years, but, as the old adage goes, past performance is no guarantee of future results.

My third concern was that the potential need for extended homecare, assisted living, or long-term health care could destroy or negatively affect the goals that they had. In good health at present, neither Bill nor Mary (or anyone) could foresee what the future would hold.

There were two other emotional concerns. First, there was Mary's mother, who, at 85, might require professional medical assistance. Mary indicated that she would want to help her. Her mother's home is worth $120,000, and she's still living there. She is receiving a small pension from her late husband plus Social Security. She also has $30,000 in CDs.

Additionally, there was the chance that when their daughter Janine resurfaced she might need their help with drug rehabilitation as she had once before. Both of these issues would need to be addressed because of the potential impact they could have on Bill and Mary's retirement plan.

Goals for Bill and Mary

MAINTAINING THEIR CURRENT LIFESTYLE:

This is always a goal for my clients. The problem is determining what that lifestyle is and what it will realistically cost to maintain.

As I pointed out earlier in the book, it's not just what you have but also what you spend. In 10 years' time, the person with $1 million who is spending $13,000 per month will have a very different net worth than the person with $1 million who is spending only $5,000 per month. Nonetheless, this is not a time to start looking to cut corners but a time to write down what you need to spend to maintain a comfortable lifestyle. You need to communicate every expense you currently have to clearly identify your lifestyle.

BE PROTECTED AGAINST UNKNOWN CIRCUMSTANCES

This usually relates to unforeseen health issues that may arise. Although you cannot protect yourself against all possibilities, you can make sure that there is a plan in place to prevent a financial catastrophe.

LEAVING A LEGACY TO THEIR DAUGHTERS

I have found that there are more people who want to "spend it all" than there are those who want to leave a lasting legacy. Many of my clients come from an era when parents were not in a position to give (or "gift") money to their children. They were raised to make it on their own. Therefore, many of these parents feel that they have earned the right to spend their hard-earned money—a concept with which I agree. Naturally, if their children need their help, they should be there, but at the same time, it is important to let children develop their own sense of values and self-worth by "making it" on their own.

Sometimes guilt drives people to want to leave a legacy, and sometimes they simply don't want their children to have to struggle as they did. Whatever the issue, I try to get to the bottom of what drives this goal. I do not counsel clients to gift to their children at the expense of having a comfortable lifestyle. Conversely, if their children are in need or if there are extenuating circumstances, I also do not counsel people to ignore such needs but to view them realistically as they relate to their financial needs.

The Plan for Bill and Mary

My recommendations are based on my conversations with Bill and Mary, the completion of the risk tolerance profile, and some computer-generated retirement calculations. There are frequent adjustments to these initial recommendations that will need to be made as life throws us all some unforeseen curves. In addition, the economic climate and other factors, such a taxes, inflation, and Social Security, will also change over time.

PROTECTION

Life Insurance: On the basis of their current assets, income from Social Security, and the continued income from Bill's pension that Mary would receive in the event of his death, I quickly determined that life insurance was not a necessity at this time in life. However, in the event of a catastrophe that could disrupt their current asset base, we agreed that they should keep the current policy for now and use the cash value in that policy to fund the long-term-care insurance policy discussed below.

Long-Term-Care Insurance: Our retirement calculations showed that Bill and Mary could live a comfortable lifestyle based on their current living expenses with some moderate adjustments to their investments. However, if the need for long-term care should arise, the cost could drastically affect the entire plan. Part of my job is to show clients how to fund the premium costs of long-term-care insurance from their current income. On the basis of their age, the approximate cost to provide $4,000 of long-term-care benefit per month for one or both of them would be approximately $3,000 per year. We recommended keeping the life insurance but utilizing the cash value to fund the long-term-care premium. This provides Mary with the death benefit if Bill dies prematurely and at the same time begins funding the long-term-care needs. Because the cash value is depleted over time, we will need to readdress this funding need as well as the potential reduction in death benefits. In the meantime, the death benefit will help offset the loss of Bill's Social Security income while currently providing the funding for the long-term care. Should Mary die prematurely, I would recommend that Bill surrender the life insurance policy and take the cash value, which could then continue to fund his long-term-care policy.

RETIREMENT CASH FLOW

I first recommended that they choose the joint and survivor pension choice option. Bill is older than Mary and statistically will probably be deceased before Mary. Between Bill's Social Security payments and his pension, their steady monthly income will be $2,700 and $3,200 when Mary turns 62. After much discussion and reviewing their expenses, we determined that they would need an additional $3,000 per month to maintain their standard of living. There is a great likelihood that the income needs today are higher than they will be when Bill and Mary are in their 80s. I always like to overestimate expenses to make sure clients are covered in the long term. Over time, income needs tend to diminish somewhat, although should inflation increase beyond our 3% assumption, the income level necessary to maintain their standard of living could remain about the same.

I then calculated that with a 5% return rate on investments, plus 3% inflation, there was a high probability they would run out of money when Bill is 82 and Mary is 77. However, by repositioning their assets to achieve a 7% return rate, with the same 3% rate of inflation, they would likely have funds that would last until Bill is 93 and Mary is 88. You notice I said "likely" have funds. Again, constant monitoring is absolutely necessary. This should not be left to chance.

Given the long time frame, we are very comfortable that we can reposition their portfolio to provide an additional 2% appreciation. Their cash flow position looks much better, and we have time to make adjustments as needed along the way. If we further believe that their living expenses will decrease as they get into their late 70s, this further reduces the risk of running out of money.

At this point, I always remind clients that this does not mean it is time to go on automatic pilot. Unlike a pilot and copilot who can set the controls and then sit back while the plane moves steadily along on course, when dealing with a portfolio, it takes constant monitoring—not only of returns on investments but also of living expenses. I explained that we would meet every six months to monitor the progress and make sure we are still on course with their overall plan. I do this with all of my clients.

If you simply leave a portfolio running on autopilot for five or six years without any accountability of where you are financially in relationship to where you should be, you are likely to end up way off course. Remember, my calculations are based on averages. Real numbers can change drastically, as they did between the years 2000 and 2002.

Change of Lifestyle

At this point, Bill and Mary had no intention of returning to work. However, I have seen clients opt to go back to work because they have had too much time on their hands or too little interaction with other people or simply because it made them feel more productive. Should Bill and/or Mary return to work, the need for the additional $3,000 per month would be reduced. This would have a very positive impact on their portfolio over time.

After all, the longer you can put off taking money from your accounts, the better chance you will have of achieving your goals and the less concern you should have about running out of funds later in life when you may be unable to work.

While Bill and Mary are now in a position where the decision to return to work would be based on one of the above-mentioned factors, there are many people who have had to return to work, particularly after the negative market conditions of 2000-2002. Most of this was caused by poor asset allocation at retirement. Many people, including financial advisors, believed that the gravy train of the late 1990s would last forever and that the stock market would never drop. The market did drop, and people who banked on their $750,000 in high-tech stocks keeping them afloat through their retirement years suddenly found that they had lost two-thirds of their portfolio. It therefore pays to start with the right mix of investments and not get greedy. Remember the saying: "Pigs get fat; hogs get slaughtered."

RISK TOLERANCE

As I discussed in Chapter 4, risk tolerance ties in closely with how a portfolio is structured in conjunction with the income needs of the individual or couple. Sometimes, depending on the risk tolerance assessment, there is a need to educate clients to make sure they understand that in order to maintain their current lifestyle, they may need to take on some additional risk. By doing so, they will not need to lower their standard of living or go back to work unless they choose to for other reasons.

Bill and Mary were very risk adverse, or conservative, in their investment decisions despite having owned aggressive-growth mutual funds and having nearly 50% of their assets in one particular stock, Astor Labs. They did not realize that at the time, this lack of diversification was indeed a huge risk. Stories of Enron and Worldcom did make them think a little more carefully about their numerous shares of stock in one company, but like so many other people, they still believed "It won't happen to us."

Their risk tolerance results indicated that they would be happy having 40% of their assets in stocks and 60% in bonds. If the assumptions, based on averages, are that stocks will earn an 8% rate of return and bonds will earn a 5% rate of return, then the average earnings of their portfolio would be 6.2%. However, if I reversed the equation and did a 60-40 split in favor of stocks, they could earn up to a 6.8% return. If they were to further include more corporate bonds, which typically yield a higher rate of return (as much as 2% higher), and REITs in the bond portion of their portfolio, then they could potentially reach the 7% rate of return that would put them in a much better long-term position.

Bill and Mary would not have enough income for their retirement years if they were to invest too conservatively, such as by putting everything into CDs. However, they are also not in a position where they have to be, or should be, very aggressive and roll the dice with risky investments. For them, it was a matter of being more conservative in their approach than they were at present but aggressive enough to stay ahead of the bite of inflation and taxes.

The first place I looked when seeking to diversify was their holdings in Astor Labs. Because Bill had worked for many years at Astor, they had strong emotional ties. The idea of selling a stock that has been like a member of the family for 25 years is very emotional. For Bill and Mary, we were taking one emotional step at a time. So, after many hours of discussion regarding the downside risk they faced by not diversifying, they agreed to sell 75% of the stock. They would then be left with 25% of their holdings in Astor ($118,750), which has been a good dividend-paying stock. The dividends from this stock would help with income.

Selling a large portion of the Astor stock gave them assets with which I could reposition their portfolio. Had my research on the stock indicated that the future was not very bright for Astor Labs, I would have recommended selling more shares. As a precautionary measure, I went one step further and put a sell/stop on the remainder of the stock to protect them on the downside in the event that the unthinkable happened and Astor started dropping significantly in value.

Note: A stop/loss allows us to authorize sale of the stock at a specific price. The sale is made whenever the stock hits that price, thus preventing potentially significant losses.

When I was done repositioning, Bill and Mary's portfolio was structured as follows:

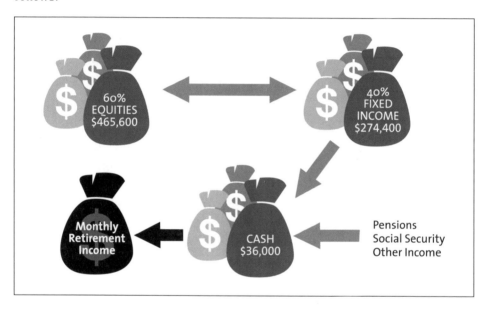

Monthly Retirement Income

CASH

The cash portion of the portfolio is a money market account at Bill and Mary's local bank. From this account, I am not interested in rate of return but only in easy access, convenience, and comfort for Bill and Mary. This is where the monthly income will become accessible for them to use. Social Security checks and pension income will be deposited directly into this account along with dividends and interest income from income-generating investments such as bonds, REITs, and dividends from the Astor stock. I carefully monitor the cash portion and the income to make sure that cash is always available for a minimum of 12 to 18 months. Mary was particularly happy that I was not investing every dollar and was providing them with secure income for the next 18 months.

INCOME INVESTMENTS

Bill and Mary's income investments are comprised of intermediate-term government bond funds, corporate bond funds, individual corporate bonds, and REITs. Each of these was chosen as a result of current interest rates and market conditions at the time of purchase. With government interest rates at an all-time low, I underweighted the government bond portion (yielding 4%-5%) and overweighted the corporate bonds (yielding 5%-6%) with a small position in REITs, which were yielding a rate of 7.5%. This money will be directly deposited in Bill and Mary's money market account so that as they are withdrawing their monthly income, it continues to be replenished with income from these assets. This prevents them from having to sell an investment or mutual fund, possibly at the wrong time, to generate income. Selling will happen when we choose on the basis of market conditions, not because they run out of cash.

EQUITY INVESTMENTS

These investments are designed to provide appreciation. With a portfolio of this size, I would generally use mutual funds versus individual stocks for greater diversification. In this case, the Astor stock still made up a large portion of the equity investments for Bill and Mary. I designed the equity portion of the portfolio with the understanding that they should not need to access these funds for three to five years. (This will be dependent on where we are in a market cycle when the plan is designed.) This allows the investments to go through market cycles. For example, going back to the year 2000, if they needed to tap into the equities for income needs, they would be depleting an already depleting asset. Because no one can accurately predict when a bull market will once again take place, it is always safer to be in a position where they will not need to touch these assets for several years. If there is a strong bull market and equities are up 15%, I will be able to take some of the appreciation to replace the cash being disbursed to Bill and Mary's money market account. This approach substantially reduces the risk to the retiree—and isn't that what this is all about?

Equity investments stay static (in the sense that they do not need to use this money for income needs) until there's a rise in the stock market. At that point, I apportion off the profits and move those dollars to purchase more bonds, which generate additional income, or I move the dollars directly to the money market account to replenish the cash. These decisions to take the appreciation on the stock and reposition are determined on the basis of our ongoing monitoring of the portfolio.

INCOME TAXES

Our plan would further take into consideration the tax consequences of the income being generated. Because Bill is over 59½ years of age, there is no reason to be concerned about a 10% penalty of distributions from his retirement accounts. However, I would balance their income from nonretirement and retirement accounts to minimize the tax burden. In Bill and Mary's case, only $100,000 of their assets will not be taxed at ordinary income tax rates when taking a distribution. My goal here is to keep Bill and Mary in the lowest tax bracket for as long as possible.

All of the above aspects of the plan need to be monitored regularly. An experienced advisor who is familiar with your needs and goals can be worth his or her weight in gold—or at least silver. It is most important that your advisor understands what is important to you and what expectations you may have.

Once I have addressed the immediate and major concerns of Bill and Mary, which include planning for potential health costs and determining their asset allocation plan, we are able to discuss the obstacles that may occur and work on tying up loose ends.

MARY'S MOM/BILL AND MARY'S YOUNGEST DAUGHTER

It's a normal emotion to want to help your family financially. A mother in financial need as she gets older will tug at your heartstrings. Naturally, if money isn't an issue, helping family members financially is easy. However, if you are worried about your own finances, you need to make determinations about what you can and cannot do without jeopardizing your retirement plan.

In Bill and Mary's case, they have some options regarding Mary's mom. If she decides she wants to stay in her own home, which most seniors prefer, then they could consider taking a reverse mortgage. The bank would then own the home, and Mary's mom would continue living there while receiving income from the bank. If, however, it is determined that she can no longer take care of herself and that it would be best if she went to an assisted-living facility, then the proceeds from the sale of her home could be used to fund the monthly expenses.

These are difficult emotional decisions to make. I recommended to Bill and Mary that they expend her mom's assets as slowly as possible and then consider Medicaid rather than risk destroying their retirement plan and not having enough money available later on when they are in their 80s. There are many excellent Medicaid facilities. Another option would be to have Mary's mom move in with them. This can be emotionally difficult unless the circumstances allow for everyone to feel comfortable in such a situation. If you were faced with such a decision, you should explore all options carefully before simply taking funds from your retirement account.

Helping your grown children is another emotionally charged issue. When do you help, and when do you pull back and let them know that although you love them, they need to be responsible as adults?

As noted earlier, Bill and Mary are concerned about Janine, their youngest daughter. Her earlier trouble with drug use could be a potential problem. While I certainly did not suggest they turn their back on their children, they need to be cautious when giving them money. There should be accountability and expected results. If not, the results may be a roller-coaster ride. Bill and Mary regret giving their daughter money when they first thought she was just going through tough times several years earlier. They later found out that the money was only helping her to buy drugs. Like Bill and Mary, if you are going to help out, make sure you help in such a manner that you know where the money is going.

Again, these are very tough decisions to make. Take time to act carefully when dealing with all emotional issues. You will make better decisions when you weigh all of the possibilities.

ESTATE PLANNING

Estate planning for Bill and Mary needed to be addressed because they had not revised their wills since their daughters were very young. Emotional issues within a family can be the most difficult aspect of estate planning. Certainly this was the case with Bill and Mary and their youngest daughter, Janine.

I first explained that gifting to the girls was premature on the basis of the size of Bill and Mary's portfolio and their respective ages. Bill and Mary, being young, faced the possibility of many things happening in the future that could alter their plans. Gifting away money at this stage of their life could put them in a difficult financial situation later on.

I suggested that they should plan for the distribution of their estate only in the event of both of their deaths. At the first death, the assets would pass to the remaining spouse with no tax consequences.

The plan I recommended included a simple will with a trust being created upon the second death. The trust provided for the IRAs to be paid out to the girls over their life expectancies. The balance of the estate, meaning the non-IRA money, would be paid out to the two older girls in one lump sum (one-third each). The youngest daughter's portion would go into a trust, which would be overseen by a corporate trustee. We discussed having Trisha as the trustee, but Bill and Mary did not want to put her in the uncomfortable position of overseeing her sister's inheritance. Income from Janine's third of the estate would be paid out over a period of time in an attempt to keep her from using the money irresponsibly. These trusts were not irrevocable so that Bill and Mary could change any of the features of this plan at any time.

The last segment of the plan was putting all of their information in the "Legacy Profile," which you saw in Chapter 6. This would provide the girls with a listing of their parents' financial information and legal documents in the event anything should happen to both Bill and Mary. It also allowed for Bill and Mary to take the time to track down documents that had long been stashed away.

Bill and Mary are typical of many retirees who are trying to piece together their retirement plan to make sure that they enjoy the vision of retirement that we talked about in the early sections of the book. What will your face of retirement look like? Bill and Mary found their faces of retirement and with a well-planned approach were able to move into this next phase of life with enthusiasm and the confidence that they would be well taken care of during these years.

8 Life's a Journey Not a Destination

Each client comes to me with a unique set of circumstances—all of which could not be covered in a book. This should give you an idea of the process I go through in developing a retirement strategy.

The decision to retire is one of the biggest decisions you will ever make. It is a decision that once made is very difficult and sometimes impossible to reverse. Most people, once retired, have no desire to go back to work. They truly enjoy the freedom of not having to show up to work every day at a specific time, and they come to relish the fact that there are no deadlines other than those they create for themselves.

For some, the stress and responsibility of their work show in their face and their health over time. A few months after retiring, they have a new lease on life and look younger and refreshed. I have seen this happen many, many times. For many, they redefine who they are and where they want to go during these "retirement years." And what an exciting time it can be. A study conducted by the University of Michigan found tha t health and wealth were not the major predictors of satisfaction at retirement but the extent of a person's social network.

A question I pose to our retirees is "If you were at the end of your life and you were looking over the period from then back to now, what needs to have happened for you to be happy with what you have accomplished?" This question opens up their minds and allows them to start to visualize how they see their life. Because we don't know exactly when the end of our life is, it becomes important that decisions be made, steps be taken, and procrastination be put on the shelf. Put your house in order!

It is analogous to our clients who when first retired clean out all the drawers, redo the kitchen, paint the house, plant the flowers, clean the basement, and throw out all the junk. You need to do the same in your financial life.

There are several reasons retirement can be a financial failure. The first is PROCRASTINATION. Procrastination actually starts while in your 20s, when the idea of retirement is so far removed from your thinking that you decide you have plenty of time to prepare later. In your 30s, the cost of a family and new home and a very busy schedule cause you to continue putting the idea of any long-term planning on the back burner. In your 40s, your career is taking off, the kids have various activities six days a week, and now college is looming. Retirement will just have to wait. In your 50s, college becomes a reality. How grateful you are that the kids are in good schools, but you are stretching the paycheck every month. Guess what? You are 60, and retirement is at your doorstep! Now, all of this is assuming there have been no road bumps along the way. So, procrastination starts young and stays with many of us. Remember Churchill's quote "It is not the plan but the planning that counts"!

The second reason is LACK OF PROPER INFORMATION. We have access to more information today than we can ever put to use. The problem with all this information is having the background to analyze what applies to you and what doesn't. I have many people who will ask me what books they can read. No book will answer all your questions or, more important, address your feelings.

The media that provide us with up-to-date, minute-by-minute information have no vested interest in YOUR situation or any fiduciary responsibility to see to it that you have a long, successful retirement. They inundate us with bad news and what to do in hindsight. Anybody can tell you what you should have bought after the fact. Telling us who the top performers were last year doesn't do anybody any good. It only encourages people to move their money in hopes of capturing some of those gains. It is unlikely that any particular stock or mutual fund will be the top performer two years in a row. So what have we accomplished with this information? Nothing, except causing fear and frustration.

I send a Market Commentary to our clients every Monday that recaps what happened in the markets the previous week. During a retirement workshop, I asked who would like to be on the e-mail list. Someone replied, "I would rather you sent me an e-mail telling me what was going to happen next week." Wouldn't we all like that!

Everyone is unique in many ways, and your financial plan, combined with what money means to you and your spouse, is also unique and cannot be a cookie-cutter image of your neighbors' plan.

The third reason for failure is a LACK OF UNDERSTANDING OF THE TAX LAWS. It is no secret that these laws change all the time and the nuances of the laws are difficult to keep abreast of as a layperson. Small changes can have a large impact on your overall long-term planning. I have covered some of the more mundane tax implications as they relate to Social Security in the book, but taxation on investments, the use of tax-credit programs to reduce taxes, and alternative minimum taxation are a few of the subjects to be addressed as you make your plans.

The fourth reason for failure is NOT BEING PREPARED FOR THE UNEXPECTED. Now, no one has a crystal ball. We don't know how or when something is going to enter our lives to disrupt the plan. During our lifetime up to retirement, situations have come up that had an impact on our financial lives, and this will continue during retirement. Retirement is not Shangri-la! Although we visualize that retirement is a time of relaxation, travel, and the time to go back to some of the hobbies we had to put aside, it still comes with the same potential financial problems we had during our accumulation years.

As we get older, we know, if we are willing to be realistic, that at some point, problems will arise. If we have planned your financial affairs in such a way that income needs are being satisfied with consideration for inflation and taxes so that you will not outlive your money, without taking into consideration the potential for the additional need of income for possible long-term health needs, then we have not done our job. Your exposure for financial disaster is off the charts. Back to the crystal ball! People tell me they will not go to a nursing home; their family will take them in. I wonder if their family members are aware of these decisions! If they are, do they know what it entails to be a health care provider?

We all want to go peacefully in our sleep—I agree. The problem is we don't have that choice. So your planning requires building in the safeguards to provide you with options if you need them. Any plan, whether it is military, corporate, or financial, should address the potential dangers that may be encountered along the way.

The fifth reason for failure is FAILURE TO MONITOR PROGRESS. I am a firm believer that a financial plan at this point in your life needs to be monitored much more closely than ever before. You don't have the opportunity most likely nor do you want to do what is required to add significant dollars to your retirement accounts after you have made the decision to retire.

Entrusting your financial affairs to a financial planner does not mean distancing yourself from the process. You need to stay involved! If at least semiannual meetings are not recommended by your advisor, then demand them or find someone else. The majority of my clients who have come to me from other advisors have done so not because of poor investment returns but because they never hear from the advisor. A commission-only advisor has little interest in working with the retiree market on an ongoing basis because no new dollars are going to be invested. Keep this in mind when searching out the right advisor for you. You want a partner who understands what money means to you and what your fears are and who is willing to be there when you need him or her and not to be there when you don't.

And the last reason for failure is NO COMPREHENSIVE RETIREMENT STRATEGY. This reason is a culmination of the preceding five reasons. Develop a strategy. It is never too soon. We prefer to see clients three to five years before they expect to retire so that we can put a plan in place that makes sense and will work given the funds and expectations of the individual or couple. Time can be your enemy, or it can be your savior! You decide.

This book was not intended to address all the issues that can arise in any individual's situation. For example, you may wonder how a book could be written about retiring and not include a chapter on Medicare or extensive information on Social Security. There are endless resources available for those types of information. I can assure you I address these issues in each retirement plan. But there are so many issues to cover, and as I always stress to everyone, we are all different. Our relationship with money, upbringing, financial experiences, risk tolerance, age, longevity, lifestyle, portfolio, fears, and family are all different. We would be hard pressed to find two people or couples with identical profiles. So no book is going to answer all your questions. Hopefully, though, I have given you insight into some of the areas that you need to consider. Understand that if prepared with plan in hand, your retirement will be the best time of your life! Retirement should be a process, not an event, and a journey, not a destination!